A VICTIM OF INJUSTICE

By
SAMUEL KATAKYIE OPPONG

The cover was designed by Prince Osei.

The entire book was edited by Dr. Frank Nyame-Asiamah.

ISBN: 978-9988-2-5715-6

DEDICATION

I specially dedicate this novel to
Maame Nyarko Emelia, my better half.

Foreword

There is no doubt that reading makes a scholar. Sadly, most people do not take delight in reading. Others do not cultivate the habit at all.

One great scholar once said that the best way to hide something from black people was to hide it in a book. He argued that the majority of us did not cultivate the habit of reading. I found the assertion rather offensive the first time I discovered it. But I later realised that, candidly, there was some truth to it. Even today, most of us do not take an interest in reading novels especially, perhaps except for academic purposes. But even so, the attitude is virtually lackadaisical.

When I made the observation I decided to delve a little into it. I eventually discovered something that surely contributed to the problem, even substantially. I found out that there was rather inadequate interesting African Literature to inspire interest in reading, especially as a pastime.

Black people, Africans especially, hold our unique culture in high esteem and would usually want to preserve the best of it. At the same time, we do not often hesitate to modify any aspects of it that need to be brought into line with modernity. Proud of our rich culture, we are usually willing to read novels and other literary works that incorporate African setting, plot and characterisation and suchlike features of literature.

I was primarily motivated to write short stories and novels by my burning desire to help enhance African Literature. And I would be only too pleased to meet the expectations of the majority of the reading public.

"A Victim of Injustice" highlights some of the African traditional beliefs and practices, most of which have now been modified as a result of development and modernisation. The belief in, and the worship of, the gods and the ancestral spirits, for instance, have given way to Christianity especially and Islam to a greater extent. Punishment by banishment too no longer takes place since the adoption of democracy.

The book, first and foremost, seeks to add to literature in general but the richness of African Literature in particular. It specifically provides insight into the culture and civilisation of the people of Ghana which are fairly representative of the African people.

It also cautions against making decisions in haste or in desperation. It posits that such situations often lead people into making terrible mistakes. In our part of the world, for example, people who are desperate to get married, have babies or get out of an ordeal often make such costly mistakes.

Suitable for readers aged 18 or above because it contains scenes of romance, violence and crime, it is sure to educate and entertain. Altogether, it is certain to achieve its prime aim of inspiring interest in reading African Literature. Once it does, I would be encouraged to continue to add to the rich collection of unpublished novels. My publishers too would be motivated to publish as many of them as possible.

Samuel Katakyie Oppong

Contents

CHAPTER 1

The Miraculous Birth of Naana Dumaa

Beauty was once born in human form in Kunso. Serwaa-Akoto was unquestionably the personification of beauty and charm. But a great deal of mystery surrounded her birth.

Her mother, Naana Dumaa, whom she faintly resembled, was conditionally engaged to a veteran herbalist. The fateful arrangement was made even before poor Naana was conceived. So she was blissfully unaware of it until she came of age.

It was her mother, the grandmother of the beauty incarnate, who struck the deal in desperation. The poor woman had remained barren throughout her married life. She had even passed her reproductive years when her luck changed. The only thing she had ever been desperate for in life was a child. Unfortunately, she had persistently and earnestly besought God and the gods for one in vain.

The innocent woman had only wanted to disprove the negative speculation about her barrenness.

Baba Sakawa, a Gao man from northern Nigeria, was a veteran herbalist in Kanana. His specialty was the treatment of infertility, and induction as well. He had supposedly helped many women who had been confirmed barren to have babies. But there was a costly price to pay for each safe delivery, the value of which was age-dependent. The older one was, the costlier the price.

Maame Kromo was a little above fifty-three when she was first introduced to the man by a business associate. She was a petty trader who traded in grains that were chiefly bought from the north. In one of her business trips to Buipe, a fairly busy market centre in the Northern Region, she happened to get the right lead while her goods were being loaded onto a truck.

"You'll have to lure one of your children into assisting you in business," Mma Kankani advised. "It's obvious you're ageing and will soon find it difficult to cope with the demands of it."

"Hmm," the woman sighed pathetically. "Thanks for your genuine concern, Mma, but I don't have any child. What has remained elusive in my whole life is having my own child. I really long for a taste of motherhood, a moment that would make me fulfilled. The golden moment would equally put a smile on my dear husband's face for the very first time." Tears had already run down her pathetic, partially wrinkled face.

"It's a pity, Maame," Mma Kankani said to console her. "But don't worry so much; all hope isn't lost yet. I'll take you to one seasoned herbalist when we meet again next week. He'll surely be of help."

When Maame Kromo returned from the trip, she gave the suggestion some thought and finally decided to dip a toe into it. But that was very strange indeed and again a break of vow. She had long sworn that she would never consult any traditional priest, herbalist or any such person again over her predicament. All the numerous attempts she had previously made bore no fruit. So Heaven alone knew why she decided to have a change of mind now that her chances were clearly marginal - practically nil, even.

The woman made adequate preparations beforehand and waited impatiently for the next Thursday. Maame Kromo decided to keep the intended move to herself for the meantime. She wanted to see results first before she would delightedly inform her husband about it. The man would be too anxious if she told him about it now. But she still harboured some trace of pessimism.

Maame Kromo woke up at dawn on Thursday and got set for the usual business trip. She hurried to the lorry station and boarded the first Tima-bound car. From the clearly deprived district capital, the woman boarded the only Buipe-bound minibus that was at the station. But that was quite unusual of her. Normally, she would make stopovers at 'bush markets' to buy sorghum and millet especially at cheaper prices. Suppliers from the hinterland usually cut down prices to stay in competition. And the clever woman had always taken advantage of the offer to make huge profits. On this particular trip, however, her aim was not profit-making. It was baby-making instead.

She arrived at Buipe rather too early and had to wait for hours before Mma Kankani arrived from her village. Time was already far spent and thus they set off on foot at once. The journey to 'the village of hope', the village that was still not accessible to vehicles, was about four kilometres long.

Bokonono, en route to Buipe, met the women and confirmed that the man was at work. She was the proud third wife of the quite celebrated herbalist. The women were almost half-way through the journey now and wished they could instantly conjure up their arrival at Kanana. Maame Kromo looked exhausted and was panting heavily. Obviously, she was not used to trekking. But she managed to stagger on at a slower pace. So more often the other woman had to wait for her to catch up.

At long last, the women finally got to the village. And whereas the southerner sighed wearily to signal her relief, the other was quite composed. Unfortunately, the man had now relocated to a peripheral area and thus they had to walk some distance again. The fairly distant cluster of cottages could be sighted from where they made the enquiry.

Shortly, after Maame Kromo had taken some rest, they set out again. As usual, she straggled behind the northerner who was used to trekking. But chatting heartily, they walked on gradually and finally got there. They greeted the attendant and anyone who attracted their attention and then joined the short queue.

Immediately upon the ritualised hand-shaking welcome, the attendant served them a pot of soft 'pito' to quench their thirst. The kind gesture, according to the young man, could not be refused outright. He said that every visitor was obliged to have a taste of the local drink at least. The women placed it between them on the bench on which they sat and apparently psyched themselves up to drink it. Of course, under no compulsion, Maame Kromo especially would decline to take a drink from such a source.

While they reluctantly sipped the drink from the small calabashes it was served along with, it eventually got to their turn. The nice attendant humbly led them into 'the consulting room' which was a distance away from the resting place.

Smiling faintly, Baba Sakawa welcomed them and then enquired about their purpose there.

"What brings you to my humble abode, graceful women?" he asked cheerfully.

"It's about my friend, Baba… She needs a child badly," Mma Kankani summarised everything.

"Well…" the man said and then paused momentarily, "I don't make babies. It's Allah who does. But I'll intercede with Him on your behalf and hopefully you'll have your heart's desire."

Baba Sakawa excused himself and stood apart from the women. Then he beckoned Mma Kankani to join him. And after they had discussed something briefly in whispers, they went back and took their seats. Then the man went ahead and spelt out his condition.

"Are you prepared to pay the price, Maame?" he asked rather solemnly.

"Anything, Baba - just go ahead and name it," she answered desperately.

"It's easier said than done," he remarked, seemingly inadvertently. "Are you very sure of what you said?"

"I'm very, very sure, Baba," she said with conviction. "I can even swear on my life."

"Wow," the man said pleasantly. "I think I'm satisfied with your courage and seriousness. You'll have a baby girl in about a year's time, 'Insha Allah'. But she'll be engaged to me, and I shall marry her when she comes of age. However, she can remarry when I'm no more. That's the price for your request."

"I do accept everything wholeheartedly, Baba," Maame Kromo said without hesitation.

"Are you very sure, Maame?" he probed.

"I am absolutely sure, Baba," she said convincingly.

Convinced of her willingness to have a baby at any cost, the man picked a kola nut from a small basket. He recited some mysterious incantation and then gave it to his client to chew and swallow the juice. Afterwards, he smiled pleasantly and said, "Do your utmost to seduce your husband to make love to you tonight and then remain expectant."

When the woman returned, she used her feminine touch to get what she wanted from her husband and then crossed her fingers. She even went as far as to seduce the man into making love to her throughout the week.

Luckily for her, she did not make a vain effort. Two weeks after the end of the month or thereabouts, she began to feel feverish. The problem persisted for a while, compelling her to tell her husband about all that had happened over the past few weeks.

Prematurely fulfilled, the couple who were desperate for a child could hardly wait to celebrate the expected breakthrough. The jubilation started even before they hurried to the herbalist for confirmation. And when they were finally certain about the conquest of the sole enemy, the celebration was unending.

Preparations for imminent parenthood began at once. And no doubt the prospective parents had in mind to show off the blessing. Quite apart from the fact that they had the means, it was the much-awaited panacea to their worries. Now, each of them was extremely relieved.

As an essential part of the preparations, the couple made plans to mark the priceless breakthrough by a memorable naming-cum-'outdooring' ceremony. Of course, they needed to take off the cloth of childlessness in public.

A few weeks after the gestation period, Maame Kromo gave birth to a bouncing baby girl. Oh what a miracle and blessing of herbalism! A message was quickly sent to the herbalist, including the day for her naming and 'outdooring'. And the messenger returned with a warning sort of response from the man.

"According to the herbalist," he said, "some brief rites need to be performed to put the seal on the baby's engagement to him." "In the meantime," the young man added in an imitated voice, "no man is supposed to touch her, except her father. Failure to adhere to this will make you lose the baby."

"Heaven forbid!" Maame Kromo, almost interrupting the young man, refused the death penalty. "We shall strictly adhere to his wish."

In total obedience to, as it were, the stern warning, the couple did not even let anyone, man or woman, see the baby, let alone touch her. They smartly concocted the explanation that the action was intended for promoting the observance of tradition. They quickly added that the overall object was to honour the gods and the ancestors of the land by whose benevolence and intervention their dream had come true.

Interestingly, the fabrication worked out perfectly. The couple of the moment, no doubt about it, even received commendation for upholding tradition.

According to an old belief of the people, seemingly superstitious though, every newborn baby consulted with

Mother Nature on the choice of its destiny and peculiar abilities. It was believed that the consultation in question took place within the first week of birth. Thus, during this period, the baby was expected to enjoy absolute peace and total privacy for that matter. Any unnecessary disturbance was believed to have negative effects on the communion and the baby's choice for that matter. Such unlucky babies, according to the belief, usually grew up to exhibit mediocrity and negative self-image. It explained that they would not easily discover their aptitudes, talents and abilities for nurturing.

CHAPTER 2

The Accidental Breach of Covenant

O n the eighth day, in accordance with tradition, a grand ceremony was held to name and 'outdoor' the baby. All the people in the village gathered in Papa Akrofi's house to witness the occasion that was sure to be unforgettable. Baba Sakawa, the saviour, was the special guest of honour. Two categories of rites were supposed to be performed. They were the naming and 'outdooring' rites and the engagement rites sequentially.

The head of the noble Akrofi family performed the naming and 'outdooring' rites. A table had already been placed in the centre of the ground for the event. A bottle of schnapps, a jug of water and two small glasses, all on a tray, had been placed on it. The head of the family, or the 'Abusuapanin', first called the audience to order and then began the rites. He half-filled one of the small glasses with the water and the other with the drink. He washed his hands thoroughly, dipped his right forefinger into the glass of water and put it in the baby's mouth. She was lying on his left hand.

"Naana Dumaa," he said aloud, "if you say it is water, it must be water!" Then he dipped the finger into the glass of schnapps too and put it in the baby's mouth again. "Naana Dumaa," he added, "if you say it is wine, it must be wine!"

"'Nananom' (or Elders), Ladies and Gentlemen," he went on, "as you all heard me mention out loud, Naana Dumaa is the name being given to the baby. She is being named after our great-grandmother who is actually believed to have reincarnated to save the couple from their predicament. And all the credit goes to our special guest of honour, Baba Sakawa, through whose special invocation the reincarnation became possible."

The man suddenly got up and waved to the audience at the mention of his name.

"'Nananom', Ladies and Gentlemen," the 'Abusua-panin' rounded off, "the rites that were performed with the water and the drink need little or no explanation. As we all know, they were intended for making the little girl imbibe truthfulness, the only prerequisite for peace and thus longevity. May we all be witness to what has just happened. Now, by the special powers vested in me, I formally 'outdoor' Naana Dumaa and her mother. Thank you."

The 'Abusuapanin' took his seat amid tumultuous applause and before long the second rites began. They were performed by the new father's younger brother.

"'Abusuapanin', 'Nananom', Ladies and Gentlemen," he said soothingly. "I crave your indulgence to speak. As a common practice in this community since the olden days, one noble man has expressed interest in marrying the little Naana Dumaa when she finally comes of age. And as custom demands, some brief rites must be performed to put the seal on the engagement. So, without further ado, I will invite the man in question to make his good intentions public. Ladies and Gentlemen, let's welcome Baba Sakawa with a round of applause!"

The man rose confidently from his seat and stepped up gently to speak to the people amid never-ending murmuring. The virtually distracting piece of gossip in an undertone was obviously about the man's background. His age was probably not too much of a bother. After all, most wives in the community appeared as daughters and even granddaughters in terms of age.

"Wow," most of the people muttered. "Well, let's hope to live to see the day she comes of age."

Baba Sakawa was in some oversized traditional smock, obviously his best, and looked very old in it. He suddenly posed manly and then picked his nose very nastily and probably accidentally. "Listen to me, all the people here, please," he began, fumbling for words because he was not too familiar with the local language. "Today, I say, I,

Baba Sakawa, will marry your daughter when she grows up. Thank you." It was as brief as the flash of lightning. And the audience that was amused by the inarticulate expression applauded him with unending laughter.

Shortly, the new father was invited to respond to the man's proposal on behalf of the minor. "'Abusua-panin', 'Nananom', Ladies and Gentlemen," he rattled off quite confidently. "A popular adage goes, 'One good turn deserves another'. For what Baba has done for my dear wife and me, we will not hesitate to engage our daughter to him. I say yes to his proposal on behalf of my little daughter." Papa Akrofi too spoke briefly, just like the proverbial Okyeame Anim.

A short moment of whispering and murmuring followed the affirmative response. And doubts about the likelihood of the inter-cultural marriage were palpable. Even the mere fact that it could be without precedent if it became a reality could trigger a reaction of that sort.

Having responded in the affirmative, the man proudly presented some gifts, as it were, to his prospective in-laws. The gifts, customary in the man's culture perhaps, included a handful of kola nuts, a pot of 'pito' (*a soft drink*) and a cow. After the gesture of gratitude, libation was poured to put the seal on the engagement.

The rest of the grand ceremony was characterised by feasting and other forms of merriment. When it finally came to an end, the man and his two companions, probably his brothers, set out on the return journey.

The little girl was well catered for and brought up. She bloomed rapidly and was her mother's lookalike. As an only child, she was pampered. She was virtually mollycoddled. But she did not have a swollen head. She was actually brought up to be very hard-working and well-mannered. Those two values had always been the hallmark of the Akrofi family.

In accordance with tradition, Naana Dumaa was initiated into adulthood after her first menstruation. She successfully underwent 'bragoro', the traditional puberty rites, after which she was declared qualified for marriage. Afterwards, her parents bequeathed all that they had laboured for to her. She was only thirteen years old now, but she had assumed the stature of a complete woman.

Naana had never been told anything about the arranged engagement all the while. But now, having been considered an adult, her parents strongly felt that it was time to let the cat out of the bag. A stitch in time, as they say, saves nine. They, however, wondered how best they could go about it in order to sound reasonable and convincing. Obviously, the old couple did not want to incur the displeasure of their beloved daughter.

They eventually summoned up courage and broke the news to her one evening. Suddenly, the young woman had a face like thunder. She did not only find the arrangement weird, but she also found it very embarrassing. She quickly and vehemently expressed her disagreement on the basis of the man's age and cultural background.

Naana Dumaa said emphatically that she would never have anything to do with the dying man who was even an alien. She was always enraged anytime the issue was mentioned, or whenever it even rang in her ears.

Although the touching story behind her birth was narrated to her in full, the young woman was still adamant. She simply found it incredible, ridiculous and embarrassing getting married to a man whose age and hers were a complete mismatch. Worst of all, she would become the first and probably the only woman in the whole community to ever get married to a foreigner.

"Never!" she swore every second. "Impossible!"

Blissfully unaware, the man who must be desperate to marry a young woman had been sending frequent notices to the old couple. He had actually been asking them to give him a date for the performance of the traditional marriage rites. No doubt he must be itching to take the young woman away. But the couple had tactfully been refusing to grant the request. They had kept tantalising him pending their daughter's consent.

After waiting for years in vain, however, he grew impatient. He felt that he was probably being deceived. One day, he visited the family unannounced and demanded to return with the young woman at any price. "Just mention the bride price and I'll pay it readily," he said. "But I must return with my wife."

Speaking like fury and sounding rather annoyed, Baba Sakawa remained insistent. His sharp contours of facial wrinkles had formed awkward designs and taken up most of his face. The man's wrinkled face, coupled with his exceptionally dark complexion and slight frown, made him look horrid in the eyes of the elegant young woman.

Just one moment the young woman flew into a fury and began to act strangely. She found the dying old man's burning interest in her outlandish, to say the least. "I won't marry you now or ever!" she suddenly voiced rather uncontrollably. "You'd better get the hell out of here!" She paused for a moment, looked the man up and down and then added quite uncharacteristically, "You awful thing!"

Instantly, the man threw a tantrum and started invoking curses indiscriminately. "This is clearly a breach of covenant and I swear vengeance against you!" he said at the top of his voice. "You will never know peace for the rest of your lives, you reckless tricksters! You deceived me!"

"And you, little rat," he turned to Naana Dumaa and added, "it's either you marry me or remain single forever, for you will only be asking for trouble if you ever dare to marry another man! You will just plunge yourself, your children and other direct descendants into untold suffering, shame and disgrace!"

"I certainly won't kill anybody," he finished off, "for I am not permitted to do so. But I bet you, I will surely take my pound of flesh. I will make your lives and those of your entire descendants very, very miserable!"

"I still won't marry you come hell or high water!" the young woman said decisively.

Palpably offended and humiliated, the man left without ceremony and never bothered the family again.

CHAPTER 3

Naana Dumaa Gets Married

The woman in the bloom of youth became very successful, having inherited a lot from her late parents. There was just one thing her parents had demanded of her before their untimely deaths. This was the survival of the family. According to Papa Akrofi, her late father, that was her maternal grandmother's sole wish on her dying bed. And having fulfilled it only partially, they felt that the onus was on their only daughter to fulfil it fully.

"I must grant the sole wish of my beloved late parents so they can rest in perfect peace," the young woman felt obliged. "They may be hovering to see it done." At the same time, she felt she had to be careful as well as selective of the numerous men who had been proposing to her every day. "They could be seeking after my wealth," she thought.

But there was one young man her late mother had found eligible and actually recommended to her after the saga of her arranged marriage. And, genuinely, she could see a good husband in the young man too. Gyabaa was every young woman's dream husband. Apart from his wealthy background, he was humble, respectful, diligent and good-looking. He was also into a perfectly respectable trade - the production and sale of kente. The young man had a workshop and a sizable number of employees who wove the cloth for him. He also had retail shops in which he sold it out. Kofi Gyabaa was simply doing well in business.

"But how sure am I that he even admires me?" she wondered. "And how do I set the stage for a mere friendship at least?"

One afternoon, she deliberately dressed in one of her best clothes and looked stunning. Then, as part of the plan, she walked past Gyabaa's shop and greeted him in an expressive voice. As she walked majestically towards the market after the calculated greeting, she flaunted herself coquettishly. Luckily for her, unaware though, the clever plan did wonders. The eligible bachelor stole glances at her and made an instant decision. He even wished for nightfall in an instant. But the young woman kept wondering, for she was quite unsure whether her plan would produce results.

Gradually, night finally fell and the expedition to the land of love was launched into at once. Kofi Gyabaa, well dressed as usual, set out alone to Naana's house to try his luck. Interestingly, he kept rehearsing the carefully prepared message with which he would pursue the angelic young woman while he was on his way. He was, however, not bold enough to enter the house when he finally got there. Instead, he stood behind it and hid himself in the dark. Then he found a passerby, a youngster, and asked him to call her.

"Ask him to come in," Naana told the young boy. "Tell him I'm in alone."

As the lad headed away she felt like rolling herself on the ground. She could not help her emotions, to put it simply. "Yes! Yes!" she yelled in an undertone, jumping a little in jubilation. "I've got him in the trap!"

Kofi Gyabaa gathered some courage and entered the house, his helpless nervousness quite palpable. "Good evening, Naana," he greeted the woman in a trembling, low voice.

"Good evening, my love," she responded romantically to the utter surprise of the young man. She quickly offered him a seat, an armchair, and enquired about the purpose of the 'surprise' visit.

"Handsome one," she said humbly and in a welcoming tone, "may I know the purpose of this 'unexpected' visit?"

Scratching the sideburns on his left and clearing his throat simultaneously, he began rather apprehensively: "Emm, emm…… As you know, Naana, traditionally, a man isn't a man until he's married. Again, every ambitious man needs a woman, a hard-working one like you, to assist him in his endeavours." He paused momentarily, cleared his throat and then continued: "After a thoughtful long search for a marriageable woman, I found none but you. You see, Naana, despite your elegance and circumstances, you have proven to be very humble, submissive and, above all, industrious. In short, I'm here to ask your hand in marriage."

After he had managed to declare his intentions in a trembling but quite romantic voice, he added, "What do you think, pretty one?"

"Adonis," the young woman replied quite melodiously, "you've actually expressed all your feelings about me and I'm really impressed. As you rightly said of a man, a woman too is often not held in high regard when, under normal circumstances, she remains single for too long. And a hard-working and good-looking young man like you is every woman's heart's desire. So let me see…...." She paused for a moment, looked the man in the face and then sang up, "Of course, I'll marry you, dear."

"Wow," the man said softly, heaving a sigh of relief. Then, suddenly and quite spontaneously, they hugged and kissed. Then they chatted for a while, sharing all the feelings they had been harbouring about each other quite frankly.

After some time, when the night was far spent, the lover boy asked permission to leave. But the woman who probably wanted him to stay the night asked him to stay a little while longer. But, eventually, she hesitantly granted him permission and saw him off. And no doubt they remained in each other's thoughts throughout the night.

The new lovers courted for a while and then made plans to tie the knot. Unfortunately, there was strong opposition. The man's family were doubtful about the success of the proposed marriage. They were all witness to the engagement of the young woman to the Gao man. They were also well informed about her refusal to marry him. Again, they were well aware of the curse that was put on the family as a result.

Additionally, the entire village had already connected the bizarre deaths of the young woman's parents to the curse. Papa Akrofi and his wife had died mysteriously in a minor accident while they were attending the funeral of a family friend. Both of them died on the spot, and they were incidentally the only casualties. Thus, the noble family felt they could not be unconcerned about the potentially unpromising union. They felt that the move was quite treacherous.

"But her late parents only died in an accident," the young man in love countered one moment. "The unfortunate incident bore no relation whatsoever to any curse. After all, the man clearly indicated that he had no power to kill - that's what I've been told. So why do you still associate the event with the curse?"

"I can understand your sentiment, young man," Nana Gyabaa, his father, said passionately. "But you still have to give us some time to consult the spirits."

At long last, the lovebirds eventually won the approval of all those who mattered in the marriage, the man's parents in particular. Ecstatic about the much-needed go-ahead, they began preparations for their marriage, the traditional type, immediately. By a reasonable inference, the pending marriage was expected to be one of a kind.

The preparations started with the purchase of some indispensable items such as bottles of schnapps, pieces of cloth, a sizeable trunk and a sewing machine. Souvenirs such as key holders, catapults, boxes of matches, cups and handkerchiefs were also bought. Most of them were engraved with the names of the prospective married couple. At the same time, invitation notices were relayed to nearby and distant friends and relations.

About a week to the grand occasion, the gong was beaten daily at dawn and in the evening throughout the village. This, apart from advertising the upcoming event, was to invite all the people fairly formally. A special verbal invitation was extended to Nana Banahene, the newly installed youth leader. He was implored to be in attendance as a special guest of honour to grace the occasion.

Soon, it was Saturday, the eventful day. Early in the morning, three Elders of the Gyabaa family, including two men and a woman, were customarily sent to the Akrofi house. They were there to formally inform the family of their intentions and again to arrange the time for the gathering.

At noon, all the members of the Akrofi family gathered in the family house and waited for their guests. Almost all the invited guests arrived on time, except the Gyabaa family. The unexpected delayed arrival of the main guests sparked off murmuring and impatience among the host family and many others. Everyone felt that they were not time-conscious.

In the midst of the disappointment, Nana Banahene arrived under the escort of three young men. Then, at last, the Gyabaa family arrived in their numbers. They all looked flamboyant in their pieces of kente. Kofi Gyabaa looked awesome in his 'Adwini Asa', a special kente. Literally, 'Adwini Asa' represented the very best of design and craftsmanship in the kente industry.

The ceremony commenced as soon as they were settled. The Master of Ceremonies, or the MC for short, asked the head of the Akrofi family to say a prayer for guidance and peace. That briefly done in the form of libation, the MC announced the purpose of the gathering. Then he went ahead and introduced the bride and the groom as well as some prominent members of their respective families to the audience. He also introduced the special guest of honour, Nana Banahene.

When the bride's name was mentioned, everyone looked round to catch a glimpse of her. Unfortunately, she was nowhere in sight. She was reportedly being kept indoors, perhaps as part of the marriage rites.

After the brief introduction, the MC invited the spokesperson for the Akrofi family to make the ritualised enquiry. Accordingly, Nana Sefua enquired harmlessly from the other family their purpose in the house.

In quick response, the spokesperson for the other party made their intentions public. Akora Pogo said that they were there to marry off an angel of a woman to their son.

The actual marriage rites followed the enquiry. Naana Dumaa was brought before the audience to respond publicly to the groom's proposal. Uncle Napo Akrofi, the successor to her late father, openly informed her of the groom's intentions. Then he asked her three consecutive times whether she agreed to the proposal. Surprise, surprise, her response was a very quick and loud yes on all three occasions.

"Donoo!" the audience cheered her on.

Following her positive response, the ceremony proceeded to the next stage. The groom's family, on his behalf, presented some items to the bride's family. They included two bottles of schnapps, a trunk full of personal possessions for the bride, a sewing machine and some undisclosed amounts of money in three envelopes. The envelopes of money, in no particular order, were for Naana's paternal uncles, her maternal aunts and her maternal male cousins. Literally, the monetary presents represented a form of compensation for the vacuum the woman's absence would create in the family.

The receipt of the customary presents, in accordance with tradition, sealed the marriage. Subsequently, Uncle Napo, on behalf of the bride's family, formally handed her over to the groom. Gyabaa gladly hugged her and then took her hand in hand to where he was sitting. A chair for Naana had already been placed close to his.

A few of the dignitaries, including Nana Banahene, were given the platform to offer pieces of advice to the new couple. The counsel basically revolved around mutual love, mutual care and mutual respect. It again touched on individual and collective responsibilities, sexual rights, procreation and trust. Submissiveness on the woman's part as well as the acceptance of members of each other's family was also stressed.

Lastly, libation was poured once again to bring the curtain down on the ceremony. The accompanying text basically thanked God, the gods and the ancestors for seeing them through the eventful ceremony. It also sought their blessings, especially the gift of children, upon the marriage. Afterwards, assorted drinks, both alcoholic and non-alcoholic, were served to both the invited guests and the rest of the audience to quench their thirst. Pieces of roast chicken were also served as an accompaniment. Everyone present, even members of the host family, had their fair share of the refreshments.

Additionally, souvenirs, including strips of kente, handkerchiefs, catapults and cups, among others, were shared alongside the refreshments. The feasting and the sharing of the paraphernalia marked the end of the ceremony.

CHAPTER 4

Naana Dumaa Gives Birth to Quadruplets

After their happy marriage, the new couple lived in Naana's house and started their married life. Naana immediately left all the property she had inherited from her late parents in the custody of her husband. Other than the house in which they lived, she had a plantation each of cocoa and oil palm, extensive parcels of farmland, three building plots, and food crop farms. Naana entrusted all those property into the care of her husband in accordance with tradition and out of love. She actually respected the man's position as the head of the new family and trusted him too. Thus, she had no second thoughts about the decision.

The man was very grateful to his wife for the confidence she reposed in him. He promised to do his utmost to be a good caretaker, first and foremost, and to reciprocate the gesture of trust. He combined his business with the custodial duty and performed each of them as best he could, leaving his wife with no doubts.

The woman assumed the position of a housewife. She believed that confining her role to the house would facilitate baby-making, her prime expectation in the marriage. She really felt bound to fulfil her late parents' sole wish. In fact, she wanted children so badly within the shortest possible time that she had to make a smart move.

Naana Dumaa devised a potent means for seducing her husband into sleeping with her regularly. She believed that regular lovemaking would enhance her chances of getting pregnant. She would almost always complain of mild waist troubles and ask her husband to massage her waist at bedtime. She had some sheabutter in a small container with which the man massaged her. No doubt about it, the plan worked wonders. Whenever the man smeared the cream around the 'succulent' waist of his beautiful wife and massaged it, he was seduced by her irresistible nakedness.

By the well thought-out plan, Naana Dumaa succeeded in cajoling her husband into regular lovemaking and remained hopeful. Soon, her undaunted efforts yielded results. The woman was pronounced pregnant by a local birth attendant within six months of marriage. The prolonged manifestation of the common symptoms, including loss of appetite, vomiting and dizziness, necessitated the informal pregnancy test.

The lucky couple who were overjoyed by the blessing remained expectant. Gradually, the pregnancy became conspicuous and before long the woman started the normal antenatal course. She received herbal medication from Nana Ama Nyame, the only birth attendant in the whole village. The old woman doubled up as a veteran herbalist. The medication took the form of concoction, a variety of soup and periodic enema. The regular medication was meant to prevent diseases as well as facilitate easy and safe delivery.

About three months later, the woman began to feel some sharp, tingling abdominal sensation and complained to the old woman. But the experienced birth attendant said it was a normal occurrence in pregnancy. The problem persisted for a while and began to go beyond normality. Gradually, it degenerated into unbearable abdominal pains and gave cause for alarm. Now, it necessitated the intervention of orthodox medicine despite the difficulty with access. The family, her husband in particular, felt that a gynaecologist needed to be consulted.

The day after next, which was a Monday, early in the morning, Naana Dumaa was taken to the Clean Sheet Hospital in Omanpon. Almost a hundred and fifteen kilometres away, it happened to be the nearest hospital. An instant scan report revealed a problem that was known in medical parlance as ectopic pregnancy. The woman was therefore supposed to undergo surgery for the foetus to be removed from the fallopian tube.

Disturbed, Gyabaa hurriedly signed the medical forms for the operation to commence without even an enquiry about the content. The morning was still cold but the troubled husband was sweating profusely. As a first-time experience, it really seemed dangerous, or rather it seemed deadly in his racing thoughts. His partially wet appearance suddenly caught the attention of the surgeon who felt for him at once. The thoughtful doctor held him by the shoulders and tried his best to calm him down.

Shortly, the woman was taken to the theatre while Gyabaa waited restlessly outside. He asked every passerby nurse or doctor about his wife's condition. But, as though it was planned, they all gave the same consoling response. "Calm down, young man," everyone said. "She'll surely be fine."

After about an hour or thereabouts, the surgeon finally came out of the theatre. At once, Gyabaa rushed to him and asked anxiously, "How's she doing, Doc.?"

"Calm down, young man," the doctor replied. "There's no need for apprehension. The operation went successful and her condition is stable and normal."

"Hmm," he sighed deeply to register his relief. "Thank you, Doc.," he said, allowing himself a faint smile. Then he clenched and kissed both fists and muttered, "Thank you God; thank you, my ancestors."

While he was gradually recovering his composure, a theatre nurse approached him. "Your wife will be on admission for some time, Sir," she said. "And I was wondering if you could rush home and bring a few things she might need during the short period."

"No problem, Madam," he said. "But please take good care of her for me. Our home town is quite far away, but I'll be back as soon as possible."

"Don't worry about that, Sir," the nurse said humbly. "We always treat our patients like royalty."

Gyabaa returned to Kunso as fast as possible and reported everything that had happened. Surprisingly, there was contrasting response from the woman's family and the man's. Whereas the former received the news with shock and pitied the young couple, the latter seemed indifferent. They just ranted and raved, reproaching the young man for his refusal to heed advice.

"It serves you right, Kofi Gyabaa!" Nana Gyabaa roared. "A stubborn housefly is always buried with a corpse. We warned you at the very beginning but you wouldn't listen. You were blinded by love."

"Yoo!" he added after a momentary pause. "This is certainly the beginning of worse experiences. Everything is obvious evidence of the effects of the Gao man's curse. You'd better do something now, young man!"

After he had been scolded, the young husband picked a few items and returned to the hospital a confused man. Naana's maternal aunt, the successor to her late mother, went with him to take care of her.

Gyabaa returned to Kunso the following morning, having outstayed his welcome in the female ward. But he visited the women fairly regularly until Naana was finally discharged.

The young man remained confused for quite some time. He was in a dilemma over whether he should listen to his family and put his wife away or follow his heart and keep his marriage. The confusion made at least the first two weeks that followed the poor woman's discharge utter hell for her. Her husband was uncharacteristically indifferent to her, adding to her trauma and distress.

Wondering what could have informed the man's sudden lukewarm attitude towards her, she made a complaint to the Elders of her family. Kofi Gyabaa was thus summoned by his in-laws one evening. But the troubled husband was neither reprimanded nor queried for his actions and inactions. He was only made to understand the intricacies of marriage and the role love played in dealing with challenges in it.

The young man realised after the short meeting that the problem in hand was not impossible to deal with after all. Thenceforth, he drew closer to his wife and pampered her as usual, and that eased her recuperation. He saw to it that she took her medication on time and again sat by her at mealtimes and encouraged her to eat well. He even spoon-fed her sometimes. Everything returned to normality again.

As soon as the young woman fully recovered, she began another herbal treatment course. This time, it was meant to prepare her reproductive system for another pregnancy. Her loving husband supported her efforts and shortly she conceived again.

"Instinct tells me you should stop the medication and allow the foetus to develop naturally," Gyabaa said one evening.

"You never said a truer word, my dear," she replied. "I really trust your instincts."

But there was a hurdle to clear regarding how the birth attendant could be convinced to see reason. The couple actually wondered how best they could approach her with such a suggestion without jeopardising their good relationship. Since she remained the only birth attendant, they knew they would need her assistance again during and after delivery. So they really needed to be tactful and diplomatic about the move. But, undoubtedly, it all boiled down to a reasonable fabrication.

The following morning, as early as possible, the young couple paid Nana Nyame a dual-purpose visit. First, they were there to confirm the pregnancy. Second, and more importantly, they intended to suggest the stoppage of the herbal medication after the confirmation. The herbalist welcomed them and offered them seats as usual. Then, as though she had forgotten to enquire about the purpose of the unexpected visit, she suddenly started singing. She sang poetically for a while and danced to the tune as well. The couple, totally silent, stared at her in puzzlement. Then suddenly, she paused and stared at the couple momentarily.

"You're wondering, aren't you?" she put to them.

"Yes, we are, Nana," they replied very quickly, almost together.

"Well," she said, "you don't have to be all at sea, for the gods and your ancestors have done it again. You're pregnant, Naana."

"That's why we're here, Nana," Naana said softly. "We're here for confirmation."

"This is awesome," the herbalist went on. "I changed the methodology on the guidance of the spirits and it worked out perfectly. The gods and your ancestors are very wonderful indeed! They gave me directions and I followed them strictly. And now we can all see the results!"

"But let me make a suggestion, my grandchildren," she added quickly. "Since the hand of the spirits is obvious in this pregnancy, I strongly feel that we should allow them to take full control over it. I therefore suggest we stop the medication until further instruction. What do you think?"

Astonished, they looked at each other's face, gave expressive signals and then answered together, "Your wish is our command, Nana."

Pleased with their cooperation, the old woman blessed them and then asked them to take very good care of the divine blessing.

The couple returned home in delight. They were now relieved and at peace. But they never ceased to be surprised at the coincidence of thoughts.

"From the turn of events, my dear," Gyabaa suddenly voiced, "I think there's cause to believe Nana Nyame's assertion. Something seems supernatural about this pregnancy."

"My sentiments exactly, my darling husband," Naana replied in an undertone. "Something's definitely extraordinary about it."

Soon, she began to feel some hunger pangs. "My baby girl is hungry, my dear," she said. "Let me go and cook something special for her."

"But how sure are you that you're going to have a baby girl, my dear?" Gyabaa queried.

"She's definitely a girl," she answered confidently. "But I won't make an issue of this, would-be father. Time will surely tell."

On that concluding note, the woman entered the kitchen to cook. But the man called Ebbe, the pet dog, fed it and then left for the shop.

Gradually, the pregnancy graduated through the various stages of gestation and the protruding stomach enlarged accordingly. After about six month, the stomach grew unusually too big, prompting the speculation that the woman must be carrying twins. Now, she felt too heavy and uneasy to walk around and was virtually confined to the house.

The foetus would leap occasionally to compound the woman's discomfort. But the expectant mother still enjoyed the painful foetal movement. She explained that it was an indication that she was carrying a healthy baby.

One Saturday morning, the woman could feel that she was in labour. She suddenly began to feel the continuous, internal muscular contractions that normally preceded labour. Initially, the unusual experience did not make any meaning to her. She thought that it was just some pregnancy symptoms. But it became so pronounced and unendurable at a point that she felt her husband's presence was necessary. She quickly sent for him and the man was at home in a twinkling.

At the sight of his wife, the prospective father could not help but rush to Nana Nyame's house. "My wife seems to be in labour, Nana," he said, panting wearily. At once, both of them rushed to the house, the old woman straining herself and straggling.

Naana Dumaa was helped into the bedroom and asked to relax on a mat. But the would-be father was asked to wait in the living room. Restless, he would knock on the door and enquire about the progress of the delivery time after time. But Nana Nyame would only calm him down at every turn. "Take heart, my grandson," she would say, "for the spirits are still at work. They will do it smoothly." But would he stop the distraction?

At long last, he heard the cry of a baby and breathed a sigh of relief. But he was still not invited to the room, and Nana Nyame did not come out either. So he was left wondering. Then some minutes later, the old woman came out of the bedroom chanting praise songs in honour of the spirits. "Hail the gods and ancestors of the land!" the song said. "They said they would do it, and true to their word they have done it marvellously."

The old woman paused for a moment, looked the curious young man in the eyes and smiled at him. Then she said delightedly, "Guess what! Your wife has given birth to all-male, bouncing quadruplets without any complications."

The new father of four was mad for a moment. He cuddled the old lady and shook her manfully without regard to her weakling. But Nana Nyame was not perturbed, realising the intriguing nature of the situation. The phenomenon that had never happened before in the reproductive history of the community was just gratifying. The new parents felt blessed by, and grateful to, their ancestors as well as the gods of the land.

Soon, the great news spread around and the entire village marvelled at it. The historic birth of the quadruplets remained the talk of the village for weeks.

The blessed mother had two different perspectives on the birth of her children. First, she believed it could be a parcel from her late parents meant to ensure the continuity of the family. Second, she felt that it could be a divine intervention to salvage and preserve her young marriage. And very probably, the second thought held true for her husband who became the happiest new father

in the whole wide world. Just like the lucky couple, virtually everyone else attributed the happenstance to divinity.

CHAPTER 5

The Birth of Serwaa-Akoto

The eighth day was the last of the babies and their mother's days of confinement to the bedroom. Accordingly, a customary ceremony was observed to name them.

The quadruplets were named Ata Panin, Ata Kakra, Tawia and Nyankomago, or Nyank for short. The naming was in accordance with their order of birth in the tradition of the Akan. Afterwards, they as well as their mother were 'outdoored' together.

Although the couple never anticipated such a multiple birth, they still had enough to cater for the babies. Friends and relations too readily volunteered support in handling them. Thus, they were never burdened by 'the divine blessing', as everyone in the village put it. The man performed his dual role as a husband and a father as best he could. Having worked hard and made enough savings, he was certainly under no pressure. He loved and cared for his boys virtually the same way he loved and cared for his wife. Thus, no party seemed to be at a disadvantage.

Naana's menstruation stopped for over six months after the birth of the quadruplets. Thus, she ruled out another pregnancy during the period. The woman was still expecting a new cycle of monthly flow when another pregnancy caught her by surprise. She began to nauseate and feel feverish periodically, but she never took them for symptoms of pregnancy. Her husband too never linked the experiences to another pregnancy when she told him about them.

After a period of persistence, however, she decided to see the herbalist for medication. She visited her the following morning and was physically examined as usual. But Naana could hardly believe the results. To her utter surprise, she was pronounced pregnant again.

"This is unbelievable, Nana," she said, smiling with cheer. Her husband too raised his bushy eyebrows in disbelief and perplexity when he heard the news. "But isn't this a violation of the norm?" he wondered.

Even though it had taken the parents of four by surprise, they were never perturbed at the phenomenon. They were even delighted that they were being blessed with more children. Naana Dumaa especially felt gratified. She believed that her late parents would be fulfilled in the land of the dead.

Shortly, the pregnancy began to attract attention. Unknown to the couple as well as the herbalist, it had hidden for quite a while before its eventual discovery. It was even more than a trimester old now. The expectant mother, still inexperienced somewhat, felt that something was amiss. The symptoms were totally different from those of the former pregnancy and seemed rather strange. But the celebrated herbalist felt that the contrast was commonplace. Explaining herself, she said that depending on a number of factors certain symptoms may be peculiar to some women or even some pregnancies. And after her nerves had been calmed, she managed to put up with any experience however peculiar it seemed.

Months later, based purely on intuition, the pregnancy was calculated to have reached gestation. The seasoned birth attendant even felt that delivery could be overdue. Thus, the expectant mother was only awaiting delivery. Unfortunately, she waited for weeks without any sure sign of labour. Now, the couple began to feel nervous. They would consult the herbalist at short intervals to get explanations for the mystery. But they would only be asked to exercise patience and trust in the gods and the ancestors.

Presently, the pregnancy was beyond sixteen months old as per the estimation. But the worst case Nana Nyame had ever known and dealt with was not beyond twelve months old. Thus, she was as alarmed at the situation as the couple. What even made everything seem more complicated was the fact that there was still no sign of spontaneous delivery. "There's always something strange about this woman's pregnancy," Nana Nyame felt.

The situation remained perplexing and irritating, fuelling a great deal of speculation. Now, the whole village was getting worried about it. Ironically, it never occurred to the couple to seek an alternative intervention. And no one, not even Nana Nyame, advised them to do so either. All they kept doing was to induce labour with the variety of herbal preparation the old woman continued to prescribe.

The pregnancy was very mysterious indeed. It actually defied all the methodology in herbal medication the tried and tested expertise of Nana Nyame could provide. But, quite strangely, the condition of the expectant mother remained normal. No complications were ever observed. And, as it were, the stubborn baby kept leaping every now and then. Perhaps it intended to give the signal that it was still alive in the womb.

A few days after the estimated twenty-forth month of conception, Naana began to experience unusual contractions in the womb. Suspecting she was probably in labour, she quickly sent for Nana Nyame. But when the old woman arrived, she said that delivery was quite premature. In the meantime, she employed the technique of induction to ease the process.

At long last, Naana Dumaa had a baby girl by a breech birth in the early hours of the next Wednesday. Her umbilical cord was already detached from her mother's placenta. Again, her front teeth, two up and two down, had already appeared. The mysterious baby girl was also wearing a gold ring on the ring finger.

The couple were shocked at the oddity, the fact that the baby was wearing a ring especially. But the old woman seemed to be at peace. "I can see that the mysterious spirits have set her apart for a purpose," Nana Nyame said cheerfully. "Rare though, babies who are born wearing such strange objects as rings, beads or talismans are traditionally special. They are believed to have been chosen by the gods or the ancestral spirits for specific purposes. And they often grow up to become heroes and heroines. You must therefore count yourselves as a blessed couple and take very good care of her."

In spite of the brief but rather convincing explanation for the mystery, none of the couple appeared satisfied. It was quite obvious they were yet to recover from their puzzlement. The expressions on their faces were clear evidence. Completely unaware of any such myth, they probably found it hard to believe.

"I can figure that your perception of the baby is still blasphemous, my grandchildren," the old woman suddenly said. "But there is something I should let you know, that the gifts of either the gods or the ancestors are special. They are always a blessing but not a curse. You must therefore try and control your thoughts and utterances as much as possible. Just make sure they don't constitute blasphemy. Enough is a word for the wise. I'm gone."

The old woman returned some minutes later and gave another message, quite explicit and divine-like, to the confused father. "Strictly confine the baby and her mother," she said. "Keep them from visitors until she is given a name and they are 'outdoored' on the eighth day. In the meantime, their visitors should be limited to the household as much as possible. That baby can make or break the future of the entire family."

"Thank you, Nana," Gyabaa said softly, shuddering slightly with a little scare. "The wish of the gods and our ancestors is my command."

Gradually, the couple had a changed attitude towards the newborn baby girl and eventually thought of her as a priceless gift of blessing. Now, they seemed clear of all the misconceptions they had harboured about her.

Surprisingly, the cute little quadruplets seemed delighted about their sister's birth. Even though they were a little too young to make any meaningful symbolic gestures, they still found special ways to express their feelings about it. They always stayed close to her, cooing and touching her restless little hands from time to time. In particular, they loved to touch the glittering gold ring on her ring finger out of curiosity. And the bouncing baby girl would usually respond with frequent brief cries and noiseless yawns. Occasionally, their mother would drive them away to allow the little girl to enjoy her sleep or have some fresh air.

Finally, it was time to end the days of confinement. Today was the eighth day after the baby's birth and the day she was supposed to be named. Her father had decided to name her after his maternal grandmother. Nana Serwaa lived with Gyabaa in another village until he completed basic school. Thus, she played a significant part in his upbringing.

The grand naming ceremony was held in the morning as usual. The little girl was given the compound name Serwaa-Akoto. Akoto was the hidden name of the late Nana Serwaa. But the creative young father decided to add it to the surname to make a compound name in order to bring it to the fore.

"She will surely be great," Papa Sassah remarked, "for her late great-grandmother was great in her time." Papa Sassah was the one who performed the rites that were associated with the naming.

Suddenly, the ring on the baby's ring finger sparked gossip among the audience. They could notice a significant departure from the norm. Normally, the ring was put on the baby's forefinger during the naming ceremony. And it was always put on it by the person after whom the baby was named or his or her representative. In her case, however, the ring had already been put on her finger. The uniqueness of the ring as well as the fact that it had been put on the ring finger instead of the forefinger was the other side of the never-ending gossip.

Relatively speaking, Serwaa-Akoto grew up faster, stronger and healthier. Her growth and development actually defied many theories and hypotheses. At three months, for instance, she could sit unaided. The robust baby girl learnt to crawl from the middle of the fifth month. By the end of the seventh month, she could stand all alone.

Now, she became aggressive somewhat, scratching and biting her playmates for any slight act of provocation. Her four brothers who never gave her breathing space were her regular victims. But the mild aggression was no deterrent to the boys at all. They still stayed close and competed for her attention as usual.

Lovely Serwaa-Akoto was friendly and playful, especially after mealtimes. She would smile like the sun, laugh like the hyena or clutch like the clamp while playing. She was always responsive to any show of affection, at least by smiling heartily.

The little baby girl quite tolerated her mischievous brothers' disturbances most of the time. Sometimes, she even enjoyed them. But she was seemingly unpredictable. She never spared her playmates her scratches and bites.

Serwaa-Akoto started walking long before her first birthday. Just like any child she staggered for a few days, but before long she could walk impressively. She even ran around at age one. Now, she became more aggressive and daring. She would hurt herself at the least parental negligence or others at the least provocation.

As she grew up, the ring expanded mysteriously to fit her finger. Although no special attention was paid to keep it safe, it never got lost. Even as she played around as a growing child, quite excessively sometimes, it never got lost. Again, it could never be stolen despite its value.

Language acquisition was perhaps the most phenomenal process in the growth and development of the little girl. As she grew up, she picked the basic, beginners' words in her mother tongue at a relatively faster rate. At about age one and a half, little Serwaa-Akoto was virtually fluent in the local language.

The majority attributed the wonder of language acquisition to the girl's continuous interaction with the household, her brothers especially. But others believed she was a superhuman character. They felt that she was probably a reincarnated ancestress or a personified goddess. Sadly, a few others felt she was probably a witch.

At about age five, Serwaa-Akoto was still the only girl-child in the family and obviously the most beloved. She was the apple of her parents' eye and the most preferred companion to each of the quadruplets. All four of them were so fond of her that they would do anything to please and protect her. None of their peers and playmates or their sister's ever beat or disturbed her and went unpunished. They were simply overprotective.

Sometimes, they even went as far as to fight among themselves for her attention. That was when there seemed to be bias towards one or another of them. The little girl was the apple of her brothers' eye just as she was to their parents. In short, she was treated like royalty in the family.

The interesting and seemingly unending commentary on the eventful birth of the girl had apparently concealed her beauty or distracted attention from it at least. No one, not even her own parents, paid her enough compliments on her unique beauty. But the mysterious little girl had peculiar physical features that really defined her beauty and made it quite exceptional.

Serwaa-Akoto and her brothers did virtually everything together. In particular, they played, ate, bathed and dressed together. While she remained close to the quadruplets, she became quite inquisitive. She would often ask them and her parents alike a number of questions at a time. The bombardment always centred on her gold ring as well as the physical differences between her and her brothers. Interestingly, she would press them for an answer to every single question she ever asked. Her brothers would usually provide any answer to a question. But her parents would make up reasonable answers to each main or probing question.

Serwaa-Akoto did everything with her brothers, except following them to school. The place called school was hell for the little girl, to say the least. She always pretended sickness anytime a suggestion was made regarding her enrolment at school. She had already attained six, the normal school-going age, but she still never showed willing. The adorable little girl who always sounded as eloquent as the parrot had no interest at all in beginning school.

Her loving parents promised her the earth in a bid to persuade her to start school. Her overprotective brothers too assured her of her total safety. But the girl was still not ready.

Proofs of her exceptional beauty began to come to light from about age seven onwards. Serwaa-Akoto was just blooming, and it got more pronounced as she grew up. She was tall and dark-complexioned. She had a broad face, a shapely nose and a very nice gap between the two front teeth. Those aside, she had dilated, protruding eyes, bushy eyelashes and eyebrows and oval-shaped lips. Again, she had beautiful fingers and fingernails as well as beautiful toes and toenails. Additionally, Ser-waa-Akoto had beautiful thighs and calves - altogether very beautiful legs.

The beauty incarnate now caught the eye of every-one in the village, both the young and the old. She was always paid compliments wherever she passed. In less than no time, the 'You are very beautiful' compliment meant nothing to her. It had virtually become a cliché. But behind the admiration was people's concern about the fact that her enrolment at school was long overdue. Now, she was about two years past the school-going age. But despite the frequent persuasion and a little coercion sometimes, she was still adamant.

CHAPTER 6

Growing up as an Only Girl-child

Finally, and not a moment too soon, Serwaa-Akoto decided to start school. She told her mother about her readiness one evening and brought a tear to her eye.

The following morning, she was enrolled at the Local Authority Basic School, the only school in the village. She was about nine years old now, but she was still placed in class one. She became the oldest pupil in the class, acquiring the nickname 'the Mother of Class One' as a result. But only the teachers and a few others could openly call her by the nickname which she never took kindly to. She would pounce on anyone who dared, provided they were no match for her. Her brothers too were ever ready to attack any troublemaker on her behalf.

In spite of the age advantage Serwaa-Akoto had over her classmates, she was still not impressive one little bit. She seemed to have no aptitude for academic work. She soon realised her weakness and began to play truant. But her class teacher would not let her be. Mr. Alansa seemed to like Serwaa-Akoto very much, apparently because she was very pretty. He would visit her at home after a few days of absence and encourage her to be regular in school. Her parents and brothers would add their voice too. And out of pity, not for herself anyway, she would resume school.

Gradually, Serwaa-Akoto managed to get to class four. Now, it was clearly discernible that the poor girl was fed up with the demands of schooling. Rigid discipline - that is, following strict rules and regulations, as well as fetching firewood or water to school and cleaning up - the order of the day in those days - amounted to enslavement in her opinion. Worst of all, she had to rack her brains in order to follow and grasp lessons.

The truant's excuse was, however, not untenable in practice. She was virtually idle at home. Her mother, assisted by her brothers, did all the domestic chores. So although she was about thirteen, she could not even do the dishes well. And it was really nightmarish when she cleaned the living room or the compound. Undoubtedly, school was unattractive to her simply because it was not possible for her brothers to do everything for her there. The clear mismatch between her age and class too weighed heavily on her.

Mr. Alansa, her former class teacher, had learnt that the wide gap between her age and class had been a real bother. As an effort to save the situation, he suggested a discretionary promotion of the poor girl to a class where most of her peers were. Unfortunately, the suggestion was declined on the basis of her unsatisfactory performance.

Poor Serwaa-Akoto continued to play truant until she eventually dropped out in class four. And despite the persuasion and the occasional use of brute force to make her change her mind, she remained adamant.

Now a drop out, Serwaa-Akoto roamed the village all day every day. She shamelessly paraded around while others were in school. The busy bee would not even help her mother do the housework or her father keep the shop. Always on the move, she had no time for any such pursuits.

The young adolescent still had the mysterious ring on, the interesting commentary on which had not ceased yet. It had actually been expanding magically to fit the finger. Now she was gradually approaching adulthood, the people began to direct the numerous questions about the gold ring at her. They had previously been bombarding her parents, her poor mother especially, with such seemingly sensitive questions.

Now, she was getting embarrassed. The story behind the ring could hardly be fathomed. No matter how well it was told, it still sounded incredible at least. Shortly, she felt disturbed by the bombardment and finally conceived the idea of discarding the ring. She felt that getting rid of it would deal with the fuss about it once and for all.

She soon finalised the decision and devised strategies for putting it into action.

One morning, she decided to hide it under her parents' bed. She rolled it across the crowded floor to the wall by which the other width of the bed was bounded. Strangely, as many times as she tried, she still found it on the next moment. It was really astonishing.

Another day, she went into a nearby forest and threw the ring away. But just before she got to the entrance to their house she found it on again and could not believe it. "What!" she yelled to herself. "This is absolutely puzzling!"

Yet another day, the girl who was desperate to dispose of her only source of problems went to the bush again. She dug a fairly deep hole and buried the ring. But before she got home she realised she was having it on again. She was outraged by the mystery.

Many more vain attempts at discarding the ring were made. Now, Serwaa-Akoto was getting increasingly desperate. She felt that the ring was probably not an ordinary thing. The young woman felt there could be more to it than her parents had told her. But the decision to get rid of it remained unshaken. "It still must go," she muttered in frustration. "I just need my freedom."

Shortly after her first menstruation, the best proof of adolescence for girls, the young adult underwent 'bragoro'. The customary puberty rites were meant to initiate her into full womanhood. First, the queen mother was informed about the experience and the fixed initiation fee was paid at once. Then one evening, in the presence of her mother, Serwaa-Akoto was physically examined by the woman to confirm her virginity.

After the truth had been ascertained, three elderly women took over as instructors. They were supposed to lead the pre-initiation rites and the actual rites subsequently. The former involved a two-week confinement and informal education of the young woman. The core subjects of the informal course included grooming, housekeeping and cookery. The rest were sexuality and procreation, and child-upbringing.

When the fortnight of informal tuition was finally over, Serwaa-Akoto was given a day's break. Thus, the actual rites took place the day after next. Early in the morning, the women went to her house to begin the rites. First, they clothed her with a piece of cloth and took her to the backyard. They had her fingernails and toenails trimmed, and her hair as well as her pubic and armpit hair shaven.

The rite of 'river cleansing' followed. The 'Brani' was taken to Asamansua, the historic stream that never dried up. She was taken straight to the extreme bank where she was enclosed by a fence of pieces of cloth. Then she was stripped naked and bathed thoroughly with some lime juice. Finally, she was ordered to run into the stream back and forth for three consecutive times. In the last race, she was asked to throw the cloth in which she was into the river. She was then clothed in a white kente cloth and carried home. The stateswomen carried her on their backs in turn.

The 'river cleansing' was meant to teach the young woman how to bath and groom herself well. A few other rites that were relatively insignificant were performed at the riverside.

The brief ceremony that climaxed the initiation got underway as soon as they got home. Serwaa-Akoto was sat on a kitchen stool and served an earthen bowl full each of mashed plantain and mashed yam. The special dishes were served with three boiled eggs on a separate earthen bowl. As custom demanded, the young woman ate just a little of each dish and then swallowed the eggs without biting into them. Superstitious though, it was believed that biting into the eggs, even accidentally, meant eating up all her future children.

The leftovers were served to the little children who were at the ceremony. It was such an interesting feast. They ate together hastily, each of them competing typically to eat more than the other. All the women, young and old, sang lullabies to urge them on as they gulped down the food. Traditionally, the generous gesture signified the young woman's readiness to make sacrifices for her future children.

The last but one rite followed the children's feast shortly. Serwaa-Akoto was blindfolded and asked to touch any two of the children who had eaten her food.

This was meant to determine the sexes of her future children. Luckily for her, she succeeded in touching a boy and a girl. And that implied she would have both male and female children at the opportune time.

Finally, Serwaa-Akoto sat on a special stool to receive congratulatory messages. The first came from the queen mother within whose domain the 'bragoro' fell. It basically extolled the virtues of the rites as well as praised the 'Brani', the young woman, for the splendid achievement. Similar messages were received from many other dignitaries, a few of whom were not bodily present. Lastly, the lovely family was given the opportunity to congratulate the young woman on the successful completion of the initiation. Papa Gyabaa, speaking on behalf of his family, was full of praise for his daughter's wonderful achievement.

The last episode, the traditional parade, took place during sunset. All the women in the village joined the 'Brani' to parade through the streets to announce her readiness for marriage. All the men too crowded the streets to catch a glimpse of the charming young woman. As usual, she was naked to the waist except for the piece of kente that had been used to improvise a bra for her. She proudly showed off her incomparable beauty by flaunting her body gracefully.

Serwaa-Akoto, now recognised as a full-blown woman, was expected to behave as such. Unfortunately, the reverse was the case. The young woman became too proud and chose to be snobbish and arrogant. No one could readily explain the new behaviour, but clearly everyone found it disappointing.

While she was gradually losing face, however, her beauty was getting more pronounced. Her secondary sexual features had now developed beautifully to prove her exceptional beauty. Her skin was soft and hairy; her face was bright and smooth; and her hips were broad, matching her cute buttocks and beautiful legs. Additionally, her stomach was flat, and her breasts were firmly protruding. Her attractive face and good height, coupled with her typical African woman's coca cola bottle form, made her a true beauty incarnate. Serwaa-Akoto was unarguably the epitome of a beautiful woman.

But could her incomparable beauty or family circumstances account for her insolence? Well, most people continued to wonder about the appalling behaviour that was ever getting worse. But the majority felt that it could be blamed on her upbringing. They argued that she was overindulged, being the last born as well as an only girl-child. But whether the speculation was right or wrong, Serwaa-Akoto was becoming more poisonous. Now, she treated everyone with contempt. Her family were perhaps the only exception.

The outrageous behaviour manifested itself in her mannerisms and utterances in particular. The young woman was too abusive and sarcastic, for instance. She behaved as though the whole world was hers. For her, the only problem she ever had concerned the mysterious ring which she still had to discard. The thorny problem of getting rid of the ring had actually remained her worst nightmare. But she hoped to surmount it one day and have her freedom forever.

CHAPTER 7

The Indelicate Serwaa-Akoto

One late afternoon, the young woman chanced upon a gold dealer, a total stranger, and instantly a thought occurred to her. She quickly removed the ring and hid it, then she followed the man furtively at a distance. When they got to a safe place, a relatively lonely place, she approached him and sold it off. But no sooner had she done that than she found it on again. "Damn!" she yelled in an undertone. "What secret at all is there about this ring?" She quickly searched the whole village for the man in vain, the motive for which was to return the spirit of a ring. She was astounded at the man's disappearance into thin air.

Serwaa-Akoto was tenaciously working out other plans for the disposal of the ring when something crossed her mind one moment. She had learnt during her initiation that it was abominable for any woman to let her husband sleep with her in her menses. "Something abominable in the sight of men is likely to be abominable, even a taboo, in the sight of the spirits too," she felt. Then, still desperate, she decided to chance her luck.

When she next had her period, a heavy flow as usual, she wrapped the ring in a used pad and threw it into a public latrine. "This is your journey of no return," she said to herself, without much conviction, though.

Still doubtful whether the action would yield results, she kept checking her ring finger on her way back home. But, to her astonishment, the mysterious ring returned no more. Now, the young woman who had proven to be tenacious was all smiles. "Freedom at last!" she yelled and then jumped in jubilation. She was alone in her room.

The jubilation went on for a while but inwardly. But there was something she had almost reckoned without. She would definitely be answerable to the family for the mysterious disappearance of the ring. But it was yet to dawn on her to concoct an explanation, a reasonable one, for the loss.

Luckily for her, the loss of the ring, as it were, remained unnoticed for a while. It neither came to her parents' attention nor her brothers'. But just to be on the safe side she felt the need to trick the family and everyone else for that matter.

"My ring! My ring!" she suddenly cried out one evening. "It's nowhere to be found! It's gone!" Then, shedding crocodile tears, she ran to the living room and lay on the carpeted floor.

"But how did it happen and when, my dear?" her father asked softly in all innocence.

"I have no idea whatsoever, Papa," she replied tearfully. "I just realised it was gone."

"Well, you can't cry your eyes out over this, my dear," the man said in a consoling tone. "An occurrence of this nature is usually beyond human comprehension. So you just have to let it go."

"Nothing lost nothing gained, my dear," her mother added to set her mind at rest. "You have to let it go."

Strangely, the young woman kept losing her diminished charm after the disposal of the ring. Nobody seemed to love or admire her for her beauty again. Even her parents and brothers who were hopelessly fond of her now appeared indifferent to her affairs. The woman who was famed for her striking beauty and charm was actually losing her glory. All the compliments people lavished on her had virtually ceased and the preferential treatment she enjoyed likewise. Her fall from grace to grass was clearly looming large.

But could anything ever compel Serwaa-Akoto to turn over a new leaf? Of course not! She remained as unperturbed as ever. She was still shamelessly snobbish and full of herself. But, as opposed to her gradual degradation, she was still growing in beauty. The peculiar quality was particularly pronounced presently.

For her fellow young women, however, her incomparable beauty no longer set her apart. "After all," they argued, "she's yet to be married, just like most of us." And rather eccentric, they felt that none of the young men would ever find her marriageable.

But the popular argument did not seem untenable. No single man had ever approached her since her initiation, let alone proposed to her. For the men, the young ones especially, Serwaa-Akoto was uncouth as well as a tigress of a woman. And no doubt most of her companions and fellow young women shared the men's opinion. Everyone wondered if she would ever fit into any man's description of a wife.

Anyone who was tempted to lay blame felt that the family was solely blameworthy for over-pampering her and giving her too much freedom. But a few others thought she was just being silly.

Laziness was now the other side of the pathetic story of Serwaa-Akoto. She was simply a loafer. She was supposed to be doing most of the housework, especially when she happened to be the only daughter. Sadly, the opposite was the case. The young woman did not only feel lazy to do the domestic chores but she also felt relegated. She felt that doing those chores amounted to enslavement which she found detestable.

Serwaa-Akoto only loved to dress and roam the serpentine streets of the ancient village just to flaunt herself. Perhaps her motive was to fish for compliments which now remained elusive. She actually felt comfortable loafing around while her parents or brothers did the chores.

She would sit back and look on while her father washed his clothes or swept the living room. And she would even cross her legs while her mother or any of her brothers did the dishes, swept the compound or cooked.

The mistress of her own affairs never did anything in the house on her own initiative. She always had to be coerced to do one thing or another. Without common courtesy, she sometimes had the guts to add her dirty clothes to her father's while the man washed them himself. And, obviously, she did worse things to her mother and brothers. Serwaa-Akoto was a real thorn in everyone's flesh.

Undoubtedly, everyone was bored with her growing laziness and childishness. "What will become of her in marriage if she doesn't turn over a new leaf?" her parents especially always wondered.

The uncivilised behaviour continued to cost the young lady her dignity and marriage for that matter. Now, she would not pass by a person or a group without being sneered at. Some people would even make a face in addition. Everyone now looked down on her, most of them calling her all sorts of names. She was branded alien to her own culture, for instance.

Indeed, Serwaa-Akoto lived on an island. She actually created her own world of freedom and alienation in respect of the norms, values and taboos of the community. She did not care which hand she used to give something to, or take something from, anyone. Similarly, she was never mindful of her utterances and choice of words for communication in general. Even common greeting, for her, was optional and reciprocal, and it did not matter who initiated it. So it was little wonder she never bowed to greet any man as every woman in the village did. Serwaa-Akoto never fitted the stereotype of the respectful and submissive woman of Kunso.

At present, practically all her peers were married, most of whom were having a child at least. The few who were still single were essentially serving apprenticeship. But the idle Serwaa-Akoto, the epitome of beauty, was yet to be proposed to for the very first time. She was clearly an unwanted marriage material on the marriage market. But whether it was real or pretended, she seemed oblivious to the situation.

Her poor parents, the woman especially, were the ones who were hopelessly disturbed by her delayed marriage. They felt that they could no longer endure the humiliation. What even worried them the most was the difficulty they had explaining the situation. They felt they could no longer provide convincing answers to the numerous questions that were frequently asked about their only daughter's plight. They were sick to death of making a mockery of themselves.

All the genuine and pretended concerns about the young woman's obnoxious character and delayed marriage finally culminated in stigmatisation. She was now stigmatised for remaining single at her age despite her physical endowments. And as if that was not bad enough, her parents too were sneered at for having no grandchildren at their ages. Just like their daughter, none of their sons was married or having a child yet. Having been unsuccessful in formal education, they were still learning trades to empower themselves economically.

But the issue about the young men was not the bone of contention. In the context of their matrilineal system of inheritance, the onus was on Serwaa-Akoto to produce children to ensure the survival of the family.

Naana Dumaa and her darling husband remained humiliated by the sneering remarks and insinuations they had to suffer every day. Now, they even had the feeling that their only daughter was nothing but a disappointment, even a disgrace, to the respectable family. The poor couple felt that the young woman was tasteless salt that deserved to be trampled underfoot. But, of course, they had cause to be disappointed in her. No parents would be so angelic as to be pleased with such a good-for-nothing daughter.

Unknown to anyone until she told a friend in passing, Serwaa-Akoto had all the while been harbouring something really laughable. She had felt that none of the young men in the village was a material for a husband. She had even finalised that the village was not at all the ideal place for the choice of a husband. "None of them is good-looking and wealthy enough to deserve me," she told the friend. But little did she know the men never found her marriageable either.

Finally, and quite incredibly, 'the beauty queen' decided to leave the village for the city. Whatever triggered the secret decision remained unknown, but humiliation, boredom or adventure could be speculated. But did she actually look before she leapt? Well, in any case, she planned to sneak out of the village at the opportune moment. She could definitely not reckon without fierce opposition from the family if they ever had a hint on the decision. Although they were very disappointed in her, the inseparable couple especially would never consent to such a decision.

Yaa-Yaa, her recent acquaintance from the city, had offered to accommodate her temporarily. She was a native of the village who was resident in Oseikrom. When she first met Serwaa-Akoto at a funeral for which she was back to her roots, she was instantly fascinated by her exceptional beauty. So she made the right move and befriended her at once.

Fortunately for the village dweller, she had saved enough from her pocket money to maintain herself for some time. Besides, she was hopeful of finding a job as soon as possible. She had probably been misinformed that jobs were ubiquitous in the cities.

The young woman made the necessary preparations and sneaked out of the village with her friend one

Saturday. And no doubt the only daughter's abrupt departure was a bolt out of the blue for the family.

CHAPTER 8

Serwaa-Akoto Relocates to the City

Serwaa-Akoto and her new-found friend left the village around midday. Her parents had earlier left for a funeral in the next village. Her brothers too had left for the farm.

They boarded a minibus to the district capital and another to Oseikrom, their destination. They arrived rather late in the evening, having followed the huge rush-hour traffic. But they still had to join the long queue at the main lorry station to board 'trotro' home since there were no taxis around. 'Trotro' was what a minibus was called in the Garden City. Murmuring her disappointment, the thought struck the city dweller to find an alternative. At once, she hurried with her friend to the roadside and chartered a taxi to take them home.

Yaa-Yaa shared a rented single room with two others in Pantoma, a very busy suburb of the city. The house, a single-storey extension, was among the cluster of storey houses by the main street of the suburban shopping centre. When they entered the partially lit house, they headed towards the boys' quarters and finally entered a 'hidden' room by the bathroom. It was a miserable apology for a room. Her two friends were in. One was sitting on the unmade bed and the other was lying on it.

The girls' room was substandard and badly ventilated. It was overcrowded and quite messy too. The furnishing, though simple and womanly, was not at all stylish. Everything was kept in the small room. Even gadgetry and other items that were supposed to be kept in either the kitchen or the storeroom were all kept there. Undoubtedly, the stranger was taken aback. And although she passed no comments, she actually wondered how they coped.

Serwaa-Akoto had two bags - a big jute bag and a medium size polythene bag. Yaa-Yaa put the former on top of the wardrobe at the corner and perched the latter on the coffee table by the bed for the meantime. Seated in the sofa now, the villager grew quiet and thoughtful. It was obvious she was yet to recover from the shock.

Now, there seemed to be some confusion about the presence of the stranger and thus Yaa-Yaa needed to clear the ground for a rapport. She soon realised what she ought to do and suddenly made the introductions. Then she went ahead and added that she would live with them for a while. Afterwards, she excused herself and went out.

"She's very pretty and elegant indeed," Comfort said to the other in whispers.

"Oh stop gossiping, girlfriend!" Pokuaa yelled jokingly. "Pretty girls don't deserve to be gossiped about." They all burst out laughing, and in the midst of the helpless laughter Yaa-Yaa returned. She was carrying a takeaway.

"Oh, why didn't you tell me you were going to get some food, Yaa?" Serwaa-Akoto queried. "I would have offered to pay for it."

"Never mind, girlfriend," Yaa-Yaa replied. "It's a welcome treat at least."

The girls ate happily together amid idle chats and funny jokes. Afterwards, Yaa-Yaa took a bucket and fetched water from the pipe that was standing tall in the middle of the house. She sent it to the bathroom and asked her friend to go and have a bath. Serwaa-Akoto was nowhere near full, but she had to pretend to be. The plate of rice she ate alone for supper in the village was at least twice as much as what the four of them had just shared. But as the saying goes, 'Beggars can't be choosers'. So she remained quiet and went to have a quick bath.

Hours later, it was time to go to bed and Serwaa-Akoto began to wonder again. She could imagine how uncomfortable it would feel for the four of them to sleep in the kitchen of a room. Yaa-Yaa laid the bed and signalled her to go and lie on it. She quickly went and lay spreadeagled on it and before long Pokuaa and Comfort joined her. After a moment of squeezing and shifting, the trio finally settled on the groaning bed.

They all lay still like dead bodies on the modest bed and were obviously feeling uncomfortable. The ceiling fan that had been on for too long had heated up. It was now producing warmth instead of the normal cool breeze, compounding their discomfort.

Serwaa-Akoto cast a sidelong glance at Yaa-Yaa and found her sprawled in the sofa that was directly opposite the bed. At full stretch, the poor friend would be much longer than the two-in-one sofa that had been used to improvise a bed. So her head and hands rested on one arm of it while her feet hung loose on the other.

"I had a full room, a full bed and everything else that guaranteed a sound sleep in the village," she said to her-self. "Is this really what the much-talked about city life is like?" No doubt about it, she felt regrettable about the relocation. But after a moment of meditation she slept her disappointment away.

The next day was a Sunday. At the crack of dawn, the old friends woke up and got set for the ritualistic cleaning of the house. It was the turn of their group and they were all happy that their number had accidentally increased by one. The clean-up, a weekly activity, involved sweeping the whole big house, clearing the walls of cobwebs and mopping the verandas. It also involved scrubbing the bathrooms and the toilets, clearing and scrubbing the drains and, lastly, dumping the rubbish.

"Let's spare her for this turn, girls, at least as a welcome treat," Yaa-Yaa suggested.

"No," the rest declined, "the earlier the better."

"You'd better wake her up, Yaa," Pokuaa said, "or I'll do that myself."

Shortly, Serwaa-Akoto felt some pats on the back. She stretched, yawned and then repositioned herself for another round of a sound sleep.

"Wake up, girlfriend," Yaa-Yaa said softly. "It's time to clean up the house. It's our turn today."

"Cleaning up the house?" she asked in a pitiful voice, frowning in puzzlement. "The whole big house?"

Her friend and her friends remained silent and waited for her to get up, the latter looking on rather impatiently. Without a choice, she hesitantly woke up and checked the time on the noisy wall clock. "It's four O'clock!" she yelled, yawning almost simultaneously. "Isn't it too early?"

"This is life in Oseikrom, my dear," Yaa-Yaa replied passionately.

"It's the usual city life, girlfriend!" the others giggled.

Bitterly disappointed, clearly, Serwaa-Akoto got ready at a tortoise's pace for the daunting task ahead. But she'd better hurry up, for no matter the length of the delay, she would not be spared the 'enslavement', as she labelled housework back in the village.

Eventually, she got set and the work began. But it was unbelievable! The woman who was born and bred in the village only made a mockery of herself. All her laziness manifested itself to humiliate her dearly that eventful morning. Serwaa-Akoto could not even perform the simple task of sweeping satisfactorily. She handled the broom anyhow and made a feeble effort to the utter dismay of her colleagues.

"She's nothing short of a disgrace to the village folk and womanhood in particular," they said to each other in whispers.

"You virtually didn't take part in the clean-up, village girl," Comfort, true to type, mustered courage and voiced. "You only added to our number. But that was bad, girlfriend."

A fairly long moment of complete silence followed the bold comments, Serwaa-Akoto's unease clearly discernible. Then suddenly, she offered to pay for the dumping of the refuse. And although the gesture could be a genuine display of generosity, no one seemed pleased about it. Everyone felt that it was calculated to compensate for her laziness.

The girls had a brief meeting, an orientation of some sort, shortly after breakfast. First and foremost, the new roommate was briefed on their individual as well as collective duties and responsibilities. They made it explicit that their sacrifices and solidarity were what had kept them as united as a family. Afterwards, they gave her some useful tips on the rudiments of life in the city.

The naive adventurer was very pleased about the guidance. She could not help but thank her mentors endlessly for their kindness. Then she went ahead and promised to be nice and dutiful. She also assured them of her readiness to learn and cooperate. Again, she promised to do any other things that were necessary for ensuring their togetherness and thus a peaceful living.

Charmed by her pretended humility and submissiveness, the old friends were only too willing to be helpful. Serwaa-Akoto cunningly won their approval and made them have no reservations about their acceptance to live with her. They cheerfully did their best to support and guide her in her adjustment endeavours.

Gradually, the green friend oriented herself to life in the city and before long became quite acclimatised. Now, she was fairly enlightened as well and could mingle comfortably with friends and acquaintances. Her friends were happy about the gradual but smooth transformation. They were especially delighted that they now found her company normal and enjoyable.

Just one thing had bothered Serwaa-Akoto about her friends since they lived together. It had actually got her anxious and confused and now she felt it was morally expedient to enquire about it. Quite enlightened but still naive, the young woman had been wondering about what her friends did to maintain themselves. She had never heard them talk about any livelihood. She had never seen any of them go to work either.

One afternoon, she happened to be alone with Yaa-Yaa, the most trusted mentor. The others were probably at the hairdresser's. Suddenly, it occurred to her that it was the opportune moment to satisfy her curiosity.

"So how do you and the other girls make a living, Yaa?" she asked harmlessly.

Speechless, Yaa-Yaa made a face and stared at her for a moment. "Wait till you go broke," she mumbled, "then you'll know what's what." And although the curious friend got confused the more, she only let things lie and made no attempt to probe. She even changed the subject to forestall any ill-feelings.

"Oh, it's lunchtime already, girlfriend," she said pleasantly. "What about 'red-red'?"

"No objection, girlfriend," the other replied pleasantly too. "You just have to buy more of it; I'm very, very hungry. Oh I'm already salivating! Let's hurry out!"

The girls hurried out and returned shortly with some appetising 'gari' and beans takeaway for two and another, a fried rice takeaway, also for two. They made themselves comfortable on the floor, ate the former in great delight and kept the latter for the others.

Just when they were about to finish eating the other girls returned. They suddenly threw a tantrum and would not calm down. Pokuaa especially felt cheated and would not listen to any explanation. They simply found it hard to understand why their friends bought them fried rice for lunch but 'red-red' for themselves. In fact, it took the intervention of Papa Adusa, the evangelist, to appease them.

CHAPTER 9

Serwaa-Akoto Falls in Love

After nearly six months in Oseikrom or thereabouts, Serwaa-Akoto was yet to make any attempt at finding a job. None of her friends too had a job, although they seemed to make ends meet. Unfortunately for her, she had virtually run out of money and was thus getting alarmed. She could sense hardship looming.

One morning, she discussed her finances that were in a terrible mess with her friends. "I've virtually run out of money and I'm wondering what I must do," she said rather pathetically. "Do I need to go back to my parents?"

"Come on, girlfriend, you must grow up!" Yaa-Yaa countered. "You're a big girl now and you can make money yourself. Besides, going back to your parents for money will create the impression that all's not well here. And if I were them I would ensure that you don't return to the city again. To be candid with you, my dear, I think the time to be fully independent is now. You can survive without your parents' support, baby girl."

"But how, girlfriend?" she probed. "How do I survive when I don't do anything?"

"With all this beauty and elegance," Comfort said humorously, "I hope to God you're already there, girlfriend!"

"None of us goes to our parents for anything, girlfriend," Pokuaa added wittily. "But we still survive. We even thrive."

"I'm still at a loss, girls," she said naively, her woebegone face explaining the degree of her bewilderment. "You'd better speak plainly and straightforwardly."

"Don't worry, girlfriend," Yaa-Yaa said soothingly. "We shall take you with us tonight."

As soon as nightfall was signalled by dusk, they all got dressed for the special outing. The girls actually dressed to the mines. As usual, the three mentors deliberately put on dresses that exposed their distinctive features. Interestingly, Serwaa-Akoto could never be tagged as the odd one out. She looked as gorgeous and trendy as the others in her satin dress.

When they were all set, they walked gracefully to the roadside and chartered a taxi to take them to their destination. But Serwaa-Akoto was yet to know the exact place they were off to.

"But if I may ask, where're you girls taking me to?" she queried.

"Never mind, green girlfriend," Yaa-Yaa replied humorously. "You'll find out when we're finally there."

"We're actually going to sell you into slavery," Pokuaa added without ceremony. "Driver, please take us to Bosco Night Club."

"At your service, Madam," he said and kept driving on.

"Bosco Night Club?" the graceful green girl wondered. "What takes place there?"

Soon, they arrived at the fun lover's paradise and entered without delay. The club, simply classy, was teeming with young people especially. The whole place reverberated gently with soothing music, most of which was totally alien to the first-time visitor. For a moment, she felt like she was dreaming. She was simply a fish out of water. But she managed to stay composed somehow.

They walked past the vast floor and sat facing the live band in separate but close sofas. Serwaa-Akoto ensconced herself in a corner of hers. Although she tried to fake composure, her unease was still distinct. While she sat quietly and appeared confused, her friends fluttered themselves and at the same time tapped their feet in tune with the live music.

"We're here to meet our guys," Yaa-Yaa whispered to her naive friend; "the men who take care of us. Just make sure you cosy up to one with your charming looks."

"Mmm?" Serwaa-Akoto mooed, glaring at her friend and taking fright. "Oh I see. You girls are into prostitution, aren't you?"

"How dare you brand us prostitutes!" she countered harshly. "Don't even dare to let Pokuaa and Comfort hear that. Do you call a woman who's in a relationship with just a man a prostitute?"

"Well, I'm sorry, girlfriend," she said, but obviously without remorse. "I didn't mean to offend anyone."

"I hope you truly are," Yaa-Yaa said. Then she turned away and kept dancing in the sofa.

Shortly, the young men appeared. They were all fashionably dressed. They suddenly hooked their arms through their lovers' and took them to separate places in the inner hall. Now, Serwaa-Akoto was left all alone in her seat. She could hardly believe her eyes.

A few minutes later, she saw Yaa-Yaa approach her. She was smiling peculiarly. A gentleman was following her closely. He was walking majestically and quite impressively.

"I think you need someone to keep you company, girlfriend," the caring friend said distinctly. She was still smiling. "So I'm here with someone special and I'm sure you'd like him."

"Hi," the gentleman said shyly.

"Hi," Serwaa-Akoto replied humbly, forcing a faint smile on her cheerless face.

"Now, may I make the introductions," Yaa-Yaa said. Then she began: "Meet Adonten, girlfriend. He's a successful businessman. We affectionately call him Rocky Fella. Of course, he's stinking rich."

"Oh stop flattering me, baby girl," he broke in harmlessly.

"Rocky," she went on, "this is Serwaa-Akoto, the beauty incarnate. She's an angel as well."

"You never said a truer word, my dear," the cute young man added in a smooth tone.

"Thanks," Serwaa-Akoto said shyly.

Virtually spontaneously, the two quickly shook hands and then exchanged pleasantries.

"Well, I guess I should leave the two of you to talk," Yaa-Yaa said and then left.

Then Serwaa-Akoto, slightly uneasy, gave the young man a quick shy glance and was marvelled by his good looks. "He suits me down to the ground," she felt. Strange, wasn't it? Well, anyway, she may have fallen in love at first sight.

"Can I perch on an arm of your sofa?" he requested humbly.

"Sure, no problem at all," she said in a welcoming voice and smiled at him.

Soon, the friends or perhaps lovers in the making began to chat informally, obviously trying to know a little about each other at least. Each of them seemed apprehensive and somewhat unforthcoming in the beginning.

But after a while they regained their composure and had some interesting chat. Shortly, they realised they had a lot in common and became attracted to each other the more. Apparently, they fell for each other.

No doubt the girls enjoyed the night to the full. Aside other indulgence, Rocky Fella actually wined and dined them to show off his riches. Of course, such is commonplace for most men on meeting a woman or a bevy of them for the first time. But, surely, the target was suitably impressed. The smile of satisfaction she wore all night long said it all.

When it was a little past midnight the women requested to be dropped off. So Rocky Fella dropped them home and returned to pick his friends.

As soon as the women entered their room, they started an interesting conversation.

"Did you enjoy the outing, Serwaa?" Yaa-Yaa asked curiously.

"Every bit of it, girlfriend!" she said pleasantly. "In fact, my guy was cute and well mannered."

"Ha-ha-ha!" her friends giggled at her suggestive response.

"You're yet to enjoy city life," Yaa-Yaa remarked humorously.

"Just keep your fingers crossed for the best of experiences," Comfort added.

"A word of caution though - you must tread cautiously," Pokuaa said, rounding off the brief conversation in helpless laughter.

It was Serwaa-Akoto's turn to sleep in the sofa that night and everyone knew it was time again to be disturbed. Strangely, she did not follow the norm. She neither murmured nor complained about the discomfort she was about to go through. She just threw herself into it and off she went. Well, I guess you could explain the oddity?

The next day, in the afternoon, Rocky Fella paid them a surprise visit. But they were all happy to have him visit them. He brought them a hamper of takeaway and drinks for four.

"Have this for lunch," he said and handed it to Yaa-Yaa.

"Wow!" she remarked cheerfully as she received the present. "This is so nice of you, Rocky. Thanks so much, dear."

"Don't mention it," he replied shyly.

"Welcome, Rocky," the others said in no particular order. "And thanks for the present."

"Thanks," he replied, slightly nervously. "Don't mention it."

"I hope there's no problem?" Pokuaa asked harmlessly.

"Oh no, not at all," he answered, looking a little relieved now. "I just called round to say hi. And if you'll excuse me, I must be on my way."

"So soon?" they said, almost in chorus. Then they saw him off to his car and returned to have lunch after he had zoomed off.

"I guess everyone knows we aren't eating and drinking for free?" Comfort, funny as usual, remarked humorously. "Someone will surely pay for it in kind."

They all giggled for a moment and continued eating. But they teased the person who fitted Comfort's description of 'someone' at every opportunity.

In the evening, Serwaa-Akoto and Yaa-Yaa had a brief conversation. The rest were off to see their boyfriends.

"So what does Adonten do for a living, Yaa? I mean, what line of business is he into?"

"He's into imports. He imports rice and oil from Thailand, and he's doing quite well in business. You're in love with him, aren't you?"

"Hmm! I'm not too sure, but I can't get him off my mind. He really fits into my description of the right partner and the right husband for that matter. But...... Hmm...... I just don't know."

"What you feel about him is what we call love, girlfriend. Somebody is in love!"

"You'd best stop teasing me, girlfriend; it isn't funny."

"Well, I'm really sorry, girlfriend. But on a more serious note, Adonten is every young woman's dream man. You'd better be fast about any move if you're truly in love. But if you ask me, you should take a chance."

"Well, thanks, the one and only mentor."

"Don't mention it, kid sister."

Both of them burst into helpless laughter and found something else to do.

A Mystery

Following her best friend's advice, Serwaa-Akoto made an instant decision. She finalised that she must have a relationship with the eligible young man at any cost. "He's mine," she felt strongly. "We deserve each other and I must have him."

The young woman spent the rest of the night daydreaming. She virtually had a sleepless night. But while she remained lost in thought she was eventually abducted by Sleep. The cunning man finally landed her in his heaven, the sound sleeper's paradise. Then he laid bare the fulfilling future she longed to have with the man who had stolen her heart.

In the pleasant dream, Serwaa-Akoto found herself married to, and wearing the ring of, her dream husband. The woman in love felt delirious to be living in the man's house. She was particularly pleased with how happily they lived together in the majestic house and how she was cherished and pampered. And she was simply contented to discover that they had four children, two beautiful girls and two handsome boys.

Unfortunately, the fantastic dream was short-lived. While Serwaa-Akoto was enjoying both the sleep and the dream in the still of the night, Pokuaa's heavy arm fell on her. The latter was trying to reposition herself well on the bed. The woman in love suddenly woke up and realised the sensational experience was just a dream. She was really disappointed and thus slept badly for the rest of the night.

Serwaa-Akoto woke up the next morning acting strangely. She was restless and completely absent. Her utterances were incoherent and she seemed to listen with an absent ear. Her friends, Yaa-Yaa especially, were really confused about her distraught state. Unfortunately, she would not open up to anyone. But, eventually, she was left alone with Yaa-Yaa and she confided in her.

"You've got to do me a favour tonight, Yaa."

"At your service, girlfriend."

"Just arrange for us to go clubbing at my expense. I must see Adonten tonight at all costs."

"Mm, mm! (She cleared her throat.)I can make an inspired guess! Somebody is getting infatuated with somebody! By the way, don't worry, girlfriend; we shall surely be at Bosco tonight."

"You're such a darling, Yaa, and I just love you."

"I love you too, baby girl."

Serwaa-Akoto was the first person to get set for the outing when night finally fell. Then she went out, chartered a taxi and paid for it to take them to the club. While the taxi was waiting at the entrance to the house, she went back and called her friends. "Let's get going, girls," she said. "A taxi is waiting outside."

Soon, they arrived at the place and hurried in. The young men were already in and having fun as usual. The girls joined them and had as much fun as possible. They drank, ate and danced while they played chess and snookers. Motivated by her agenda to impress the man and win his heart, Serwaa-Akoto actually stole the spotlight. She looked smart and stunning in her skimpy pink dress and red high heels. She was graceful as usual and naturally responsive to the man's romantic gestures. No wonder he proposed to her and made her feel relieved and ecstatic all night long.

The woman who was clearly infatuated with the man and had remained expectant accepted the proposal in a singsong tone. But the affirmative answer was not without the norm - the usual, pretended, womanish hesitation.

When all of them had gathered in the inner hall for their final goodbyes, Rocky Fella seized the moment to let the cat out of the bag.

"Excuse me, Ladies and Gentlemen," he said softly, "I've got great news to share. Serwaa-Akoto and I are now lovers. In fact, we're one flesh. You may call us Romeo and Juliet."

"Hear! Hear!" they yelled in chorus in approval of the relationship.

"Now, let's drink to your new-found love!" one of the young men proposed a toast and everyone drank it to the new lovers.

The new lovers arranged to go out on a date in three days' time. The young man would pick the young woman up around six O'clock in the evening.

Serwaa-Akoto was about twenty-six and still a virgin. Thus, concerning issues about relationships, she was as naive as a toddler. So, as usual, she discussed her imminent date with her favourite mentor and sought her guidance.

"So what does a normal date involve, Yaa?"
"It's fun-packed, I should say. It usually involves eating and drinking, sharing of ideas and perhaps some secrets, and maybe sex."
"What! Did you say sex?"
"Yes, I did, girlfriend. It sometimes forms an important part of a date. Some men will always insist on it."
"So what's the first experience like?"

"Well, it's quite painful in the beginning, especially for virgins like you. But the pain gradually subsides and it may turn out to be romantic and enjoyable."

"Mmm? So what do I do if he makes the move?"

"You love him, don't you?"

"Of course, I do."

"Well, just say no on the first occasion and tell him you're still a virgin. But if he should insist, like most men do, you may yield. But even so, you must be chaste in your responses."

"Hmm, I'll just try my best, Yaa. Thank you so much."

"Don't mention it, girlfriend."

On the night of the rendezvous, Serwaa-Akoto got ready as early as possible and waited impatiently for the man. She even refused supper in the hope that she would have her favourite at her date. She was immaculately dressed and she looked gorgeous as usual. But she needed to ask her mentor a few other things.

"So how do I make him a happy man, Yaa?" she asked rather naively. "And how do I make the night one to remember?"

"Just be confident, lively and polite," she replied cheerfully. "And don't unnecessarily refuse anything he offers you even if you aren't interested. Be romantic and responsive as well, but modesty should be your watchword."

The women were yet to round off the conversation when they heard a gentle knock on the door. At once, they guessed who the person must be and quickly put a few things in order again. "Come in, please," they said together in the sweetest feminine voice.

Serwaa-Akoto rose quickly to meet him as soon as he appeared. They shot glances at each other, smiled and then hugged.

"You look stunning, dear," Adonten gave a compliment.

"Thank you, darling," she said and then returned the compliment. "You look stunning too."

"Thanks," the young man said briefly.

After the brief exchange of pleasantries they said goodbye to Yaa-Yaa and left. A few minutes later, they were at the Garden of Eden Hotel. The lovers had the fun of their lives that eventful night. They ate delicious meals, drank sumptuous exotic wines and played a lot of interesting games. Rocky Fella had expensive tastes aside from his intent on making an impression on his lover.

Later, they sat by the pool and had a heart-to-heart.

"Would you mind if we passed the night here, sweetheart?"

"Well, not really, dear, only I didn't tell my friends I'd pass the night. They'll be expecting me back."

"Come on, baby, you don't need to tell them everything. Once you're with me, they definitely know you're safe."
"OK, darling, I wouldn't mind."
"Ahaa! Do we now have a deal?"
"Yes, we do, darling."
"That's my baby!"

At once, Rocky Fella booked a suite and remained expectant. Afterwards, they had some more interesting chat. While the man sipped glasses of red wine to boost his stamina perhaps, the woman struggled with just a glass of sweet white wine.

When it was almost midnight they left the poolside and went to their suite. It was a three-room penthouse suite on the third floor. Soon after they had had a simultaneous quick shower at separate bathrooms, the romance began. Rocky Fella initiated the drama with romantic touches to which Serwaa-Akoto responded with chaste kisses and cuddles.

Gradually, the young man was getting there. The foreplay went on for a while and the man's organ was noticeably erect. Realising he was now in the mood, Serwaa-Akoto interrupted politely and romantically.

"Do you know I'm still a virgin, Rocky?"
"A virgin? Are you sure?"

"Yes, darling, I'm very sure. No man has ever slept with me before."

"Wow! This is incredible! I'm proud of you, Serwaa. You've really impressed me and pulled at my heartstrings. And I cross my heart, sweetheart, you're the only woman in my life henceforth. I love you so dearly, Serwaa."

"I love you so dearly too, Rocky."

"Then prove it tonight, baby. Prove that you truly love me and let me sleep with you. Make me the hero in your love story and I'll forever love and cherish you."

"I'm all yours, my dear. My whole being, including my virginity, is all yours tonight. I really love you, Rocky."

Instantly, the foreplay resumed and gradually got to its peak. Now, both of them were clearly in the mood. Almost spontaneously, they stripped naked and were poised for action. But when the curious young man finally made the move, he suddenly lost erection and never regained it all night long. None of the several desperate attempts both of them made could make the anxious young man regain his potency. He remained speechless with humiliation while the woman remained puzzled and probably traumatised.

CHAPTER 11

The Breakup

As soon as she got home the following morning, she gave a blow-by-blow account of the strange experience to her mentor. Yaa-Yaa could hardly believe the narrative. But she quickly hid her sincere feelings about it and tried her utmost to make it appear less unnatural.

"You don't have to worry about it, girlfriend," she said. "Such an experience is not uncommon with first dates, especially on the man's part. Even your mere nakedness could cause his plans to blow up in his face. He'll surely overcome it some other time."

"Sure?" she wondered.

"Trust me, girlfriend," the good friend maintained. "It was just a complex and I'm sure he'll overcome it next time."

Adonten took his courage in both hands and paid Serwaa-Akoto an unexpected visit in the evening. It was definitely a move to help him overcome the feeling of embarrassment that still hung over him. Quite trauma-tised, the woman had refused to go out with her friends and thus they had their privacy to talk. And although the conversation made no reference to the terrible experience, it was clearly to each other's relief. At least it helped to clear their nagging doubts.

A while later, the other girls returned home. They unintentionally got involved in the lovers' conversation, changed the tempo and made it exciting. Previous to the intrusion, it was such a lifeless thing.

Getting to the tail end of the lively chat, the gregarious Pokuaa, the funniest of all, asked a teaser jokingly. "So, which of us would you choose for a lover besides your beautiful queen, Rocky?" she said. "Would it probably be the slender Yaa-Yaa, or the fair, blonde Comfort, or me, your baby's lookalike?"

Clearly, none of them could help the laughter. But as soon as they recovered their composure, the young man asked permission and left.

About a fortnight later, Serwaa-Akoto visited her boyfriend in his house. It was a fixed visit. Yaa-Yaa played a mediating role by taking her baby of a friend to the man's house. But after a special, dignifying welcome treat, Yaa-Yaa returned home and left the lovebirds to fate.

The lovers really enjoyed the romantic moment. They had a cosy heart-to-heart that was almost climaxed by lovemaking by mutual agreement. But, strangely again, the lover boy who was anxious to break the young woman's virginity lost erection at the point of insertion.

"Something must definitely be wrong somewhere!" he voiced in annoyance. "You may be married spiritually, Serwaa." He was clearly frustrated.

Tears of spontaneous emotion kept running down her innocent face that was clouded over in puzzlement. "Oh why, Fate?" she said to herself. "Why have you dealt me this cruel blow?" Of course, she could sense danger. The signs were as clear as day.

A while later, obviously out of humiliation, Serwaa-Akoto requested to be dropped off. But the young man who had since remained quiet pretended as though he did not hear anything. But the request was made again and now he hesitantly got dressed and then signalled his readiness. The woman who was still in silent tears managed to put on a cheerful face and afterwards they left the room.

Blissfully unaware, the young man was up to something in that quiet mood. He suddenly parked at the roadside, under a mango tree, and rested his head on the steering wheel. Then he sighed twice consecutively and shook his head pathetically at the same time. Clearly, his heart was aching.

Serwaa-Akoto was now a chick in the cold. Her nervousness was palpably discernible. She could see trouble looming.

"Is anything the matter, sweetheart?"

"Well, I'm afraid we'll have to break up now. I don't think I can endure the humiliation any longer."

"But you can't do this to me, Rocky. You know I love you so dearly. You're the first man in my whole love life and I can't afford to lose you. Don't break my heart, please."

"I love you so dearly too, Serwaa, I sincerely do. Unfortunately, this is a matter of life and death!"

"You've definitely got a point, baby, I don't dispute that. But I still think you're not being fair to me. It isn't my fault, dear."

"It isn't your fault? Well, maybe you're right. But may I ask who takes the blame?"

"You don't have to misconstrue me, sweetheart. This certainly can't be the moment to blame."

"Well, my dear, my mind's made up and nothing will make me change it. I think the earlier you came to terms with the reality the better."

Now, Serwaa-Akoto was a dead body in her seat. She remained dumb and still until she was finally dropped off. The sudden breakup and the bizarre cause of it were nothing short of a bitter pill to swallow. The worst of it was, the young man sternly warned her against bothering him again.

At this particular moment, Serwaa-Akoto was mad with grief. She could hardly control the raining tears as she waved goodbye to the man she was madly in love with. To avoid attracting attention and arousing suspicion, however, she managed to feign composure before entering the house. Unfortunately, the comforter was not at home yet. And momentarily she felt like ending it all and shaming destiny. She even wished for the presence of the others so she could share the bad news. The poor woman who was depressed desperately needed to talk to someone.

Confused, she sprawled in the sofa, rested her heavy head on the shrunk armrest and shed helpless tears. Then suddenly, she heard a knock on the door. Guessing that maybe the man had had a change of mind and come back for reconciliation, there was some slight mood swing. She hurriedly opened the door to meet the man after her heart, only to discover that she had guessed wrongly. Far from her expectations, it was her friends who had returned. Fairly suspicious, they had departed from the norm and knocked because the door was shut. Normally, it was left ajar.

The disappointment was the straw that broke the camel's back. Virtually sobbing now, the dumped, broken-hearted woman ran back and lay restlessly in the sofa. At once, Yaa-Yaa had the suspicion that the strange experience had recurred and possibly resulted in a breakup. But she managed to hide the feeling and quickly pretended to be confused. The other girls looked bewildered too.

Pokuaa: "What's wrong, baby girl? This is so unlike you."
Comfort: "Just calm down, wipe your tears and talk to us. You must talk to us, girlfriend."
Yaa-Yaa: "A problem is partially solved when it is shared, girlfriend. You must talk to us."
Serwaa-Akoto: "He's dumped me, the only man in my life has just dumped me."

Serwaa-Akoto went on to narrate the shocking details of the breakup to her friends, including all that had happened previously. Empathetic, they gazed at her in disbelief as she recounted the appalling experience in uncontrollable tears.

"Painful though, you shouldn't worry about it so much, Serwaa," Yaa-Yaa said in silent tears. "When one door closes, another surely opens."

"Adonten was certainly not your Adam, girlfriend," Pokuaa chipped in softly. "The man whose rib was used to form you will surely come knocking on your door."

"Just dry your precious tears, baby girl," Comfort said to round off everything. "Although heard melodies are sweet, those unheard are usually sweeter. You'll surely meet the best man one day."

Serwaa-Akoto went to bed on an empty stomach and had a sleepless night as a result of the unpleasant experience. She woke up very late the following morning. She slept away virtually all the morning and perhaps most of her troubles. Her friends were not around when she woke up. They were very probably at the hairdresser's.

She lazily freshened up, turned on the television and sat before it. But she could hardly concentrate her attention on the programme. Soon, it was lunchtime. And although she had not eaten anything since morning, she was not feeling hungry. A while later, she felt that she must eat something to forestall any stomach trouble. But the seemingly treacherous weather was quite demotivating.

She finally had a bath, got dressed and set off to Sankofa, the 'chop bar' of the moment. The special local food outlet was off the next street. As usual, she walked quite slowly and gracefully along the pavement, facing the oncoming traffic. The high street was always busy and dangerous, especially during the day.

The young woman was perhaps the luckiest person in the whole wide world on that day. She only narrowly escaped death while she was rounding the sharp curve beyond which the route that branched off the next street to the 'chop bar' lay. A four-wheel drive Mercedes Benz that was speeding steadily nearly knocked her down.

The awkward beggar by the roadside had been provoked and was indiscriminately hurling insults at every passerby. The laughable scene captivated most people and the troubled Serwaa-Akoto was without exception. Despite her burden of disappointment, she could hardly help laughing. Unfortunately, she lost herself in the laughter and did not realise she had gone beyond the pavement and into the outer lane.

The driver, frightened, stopped at a safe place at once. Then he hurriedly got off the car and rushed to see if all was well with the woman. He was a well-dressed, good-looking young man. Having been scared to death, Serwaa-Akoto was still shuddering.

"Sorry for frightening you, pretty one."

"That's all right, Sir. It wasn't even your doing. I should rather apologise for my misbehaviour as a pedestrian. I'm really sorry, Sir."

"No, my dear, you can't take the blame. I'm to blame for everything. At least I should have been watchful. By the way, my name is Joe Boye. I live in Germany."

"I'm Serwaa-Akoto."

"Pleased to meet you, Serwaa."

"Pleased to meet you too, Joe."

"But I was wondering if I could pay you a visit tonight?"

"Tonight? Why not tomorrow or some other time, Joe?"

"It'll be a harmless visit, my dear. Let's just say it's meant to check on you."

"Well, if you insist. I live in Achaw Memorial House. It's up the street, adjacent to Picorna Spot. I'll be expecting you then."

"All right. See you later, dear."

"See you later, Joe."

Actions, as they say, speak louder than words. Judging by the young man's wordless expressions in particular, the woman could see his intentions. She could understand that he had fallen for her. And no doubt she fancied him too. In fact, the undeniable attraction between the two could be sensed.

When she got home, she could not wait to tell her friends about the great news that had emerged from what could have been a bit of sad news. Although she was hungry now and the same could hold true for the others, she still insisted on sharing it first. She jokingly hid the food under the bed and craved their attention. And when everyone was all ears, she rattled through heartily.

"We told you the sea never dries up!" Yaa-Yaa remarked happily. "But how could you be selling all this beauty and charm at a loss? Listen, girlfriend, if you lose a hundred of them, a thousand will come knocking on your door."

"Wow!" Pokuaa said teasingly. "I really feel proud to be talking to a would-be German 'borgar'. All right for some people!"

"The only person I envy in this whole wide world is you, girlfriend," Comfort added. "You always get the best of everything. Indeed, it's a privilege to be naturally adorned."

On that praising note, they all giggled and then had lunch amid unending guesses about what the future held for the lucky girl. Afterwards, the other girls had siesta while Serwaa-Akoto washed some bedding.

A Nine-day Wonder

Gradually, the sun went down and evening approached. Serwaa-Akoto was getting increasingly excited now. There was demonstrable impatience in her eyes. By six O'clock, she was all set to welcome the German 'borgar'. For the sake of curiosity, her friends decided to spend part of the evening at home in order to meet the special visitor.

Unfortunately, they waited anxiously for hours in vain. Now, the other girls were disenchanted. They felt they could tolerate the waste of their precious time only so far and no further. But Serwaa-Akoto was still hopeful. She felt that the gentleman could never disappoint her. So she reasoned with her friends to stay a little while longer. "You have to meet him and compare him with the ex," she said.

About half an hour later, when every hope for the man's arrival was virtually lost, the girls refused to be persuaded.

"We're gone to have fun," they said together teasingly. "You can keep waiting in vain."

"Women of little faith and patience," she replied humorously. "You'll never meet the bridegroom."

"Don't mind us, girlfriend," Yaa-Yaa said. "And never say die."

Finally, they said goodbye to her and left. But right at the entrance to the house they met a man, a real gentleman, and quickly hazarded a guess at who he could be. After showing common courtesy by greeting them, they helped him.

Pokuaa: "You must be Joe Boye, Sir?"
Man: "Yes, I am. But how did you know my name?"
Pokuaa: "We're Serwaa-Akoto's friends. She's been expecting you."
Joe Boye: "Oh, I see."

The man was led in to meet the young woman who had remained anxious to welcome him. She gave him a warm hug and quickly offered him a seat. Then, humbly, she made the introductions. "Please, meet my friends who are more or less sisters to me," she said with a smile. "This is Yaa-Yaa, this is Pokuaa and this is Comfort. Girls, this is Joe Boye, the man I told you about."

"Pleased to meet you, Joe," the girls said together pleasantly.

"Pleased to meet you too, angels," he replied cheerfully.

After the brief introductions the others excused themselves and left. Now, Serwaa-Akoto and her special visitor were alone in the room. Before long, the heart-to-heart got underway. The man first found out about how she was doing. Then, without hesitation, he hit the nail on the head regarding his feelings about the young woman. She simply personified beauty and grace in his restless eyes.

"I returned home for the sole purpose of looking for a wife and getting married. But until we met, I had harboured the feeling that I had made a vain journey. Although my days are numbered, I must get married before I finally leave for Germany. My parents especially will be at peace if this dream comes true. Will you marry me, angel?"

"Hmm, this is really unexpected. I actually don't know what I should say. But are you serious, Joe? I mean, is marriage a sure thing?"

"Yes, it is, sweetheart. I can even swear on my life if you wish. I'm ready to meet your parents any day, even tomorrow, and marry you at your convenience."

"This is utter seriousness!"

"I'm dead serious, sweetheart."

"I think I'm convinced. I'll marry you, Joe."

"Wow! Thanks for giving me the chance to love you, Serwaa. I'll pick you up tomorrow morning to meet my parents."
"Are you that serious, Joe?"
"I'm a man of my word."

After the agreement, the new lovers went on to have some more intimate chat. It was definitely the moment to find out more about each other. The woman especially was more curious. Ostensibly, she wanted to know more about his life abroad. Later, when it was getting too late, the 'borgar' requested permission to leave. But it took quite a while for the woman who was absolutely delighted with the visit, the proposal especially, to grant the request and see him off.

Shortly, her friends returned. They were all itching to listen to whatever had happened between the lovers. It appeared their friend too was eager to tell them the lovers' tale. But someone needed to squeeze the trigger. And as soon as Yaa-Yaa did, she went ahead and told them everything. Then she quickly found out how they felt about the acceptance of the proposal.

Serwaa-Akoto: "Do you think I made the right decision by accepting to marry him?"
Pokuaa: "You made the best decision, girlfriend. After all, marriage, a good one of course, like the

one we'll witness pretty soon, gives every woman some sense of pride."

Comfort: "My sentiments exactly, my dear. He's rich and good-looking. And he appears to be TLC - tender, loving and caring. What else does a woman expect of a husband, girlfriend?"

Yaa-Yaa: "You always get the best, Serwaa. It's indeed good to be born beautiful and charming."

Serwaa-Akoto: Well, guess what, girls? I'm meeting his parents tomorrow morning. And after their approval, I'll take him to Kunso to meet my parents too."

Pokuaa: "Wow! So soon? I'm really happy for you, girlfriend."

Serwaa-Akoto: "He wants everything done as soon as possible. His days in Ghana are numbered."

Yaa-Yaa: "But I hope he's going back to Germany with you? Of course, it'll be too risky to leave a beautiful wife like you behind."

Comfort: "You never said a truer word, Yaa. He must return with her at all costs."

The sentimental comments about the seemingly imminent marriage went on for a while. Then suddenly, the conversation took on a whole new dimension. Direct comparison between the new boyfriend and the former became the new subject. And by the time it was exhausted, the former boyfriend had been branded callous and painted a caricature. They finally got onto the subject of working abroad. But before they could do justice to it, Sleep, the cunning man, paid them a surprise visit and took them to his heaven one after the other.

Joe Boye and his new-found lover went to meet his parents the following morning. The graceful old couple were instantly fascinated by her looks. Suitably impressed by her manners as well, especially her humility, they gave their consent to the proposed marriage almost immediately.

"My grandchildren will surely be cute boys and girls," Enoma Pomaa, the lovely old woman, remarked briefly.

"Indeed, my son has good taste," his father said. "This is certainly the best choice."

"Like father like son," Enoma added.

"You'll soon be living with us until you join him in Germany," Nana Dogo said, and that rounded off the conversation.

The lovers met the following day and decided to visit the woman's parents the day after next to seek their consent too. It was a Friday and it happened to be the day Patapaa and his local band were organising a concert at Lobito, the new cinema. Joe Boye and his fiancée decided to attend the show and agreed to spend the night together afterwards.

The young woman and her friends were picked up for supper at a classy restaurant around half past five. Afterwards, they drove straight to Lobito and attended the concert together. They had a nice time singing and dancing as well as laughing and cheering heartily. The good show was climaxed by an absorbing drama that was performed near the end. The party certainly found the show worthwhile. The ladies especially enjoyed every bit of it and went home fully satisfied.

The lovebirds first dropped the three ladies off and then went to the man's place to spend the night. The concert had already put them in the right mood. Thus, it was as easy as blinking reviving it after freshening up. Serwaa-Akoto had already mentioned her virginity to the young man in passing. So he was only too eager to become the hero in her love story.

Shortly, both of them felt in the mood and could not help it. Then the young man who was curious to have a taste of a virgin made an attempt to make love to her and proudly break her virginity. Sadly, and rather mysteriously, the 'borgar' too lost erection at the point of insertion.

"It's my fault," she felt. "I'm the problem. He's totally blameless." She could actually feel it in her bones.

Assisted by the naive woman somehow, the man who appeared a little embarrassed now made several unsuccessful attempts at regaining erection. Then, unaware of the secret, he conceded having a complex of some sort inwardly. Suddenly, he was struck by a thought. "The dawn is the surest moment for erection for every man," he said persuasively. "So I guess we should postpone everything until the crack of dawn."

Poor Serwaa-Akoto breathed a sigh of relief when the postponement was suggested. However, she was least hopeful things would work in her favour. She only kept her fingers crossed for a miracle as both of them tried to sleep their worries away.

Joe Boye was pretty sure the alarm clock would wake him up for the encounter. Besides, the bells of the nearby church would ring as usual.

Just as he had hoped, he was awoken in plenty of time. Then, very romantically, he woke his partner up and tried to put her in the mood. Now, he was at the peak of erection and very optimistic of success. A few minutes later, the mood took the woman too and both of them were poised for real action. With the best of appetite now, the man decided to eat the early morning cake hot. He made a fairly gentle effort to bite into it, only to be humiliated again. While he was getting closer, he suddenly lost erection. Then, obviously, he lost all his patience too.

"This is very uncharacteristic of my sexual experiences," he voiced rather harshly. "I strongly believe that something is wrong with you. Just get dressed and let me drop you off. We'll talk about it later."

Later, when his parents had woken up, he discussed the bizarre experience with them and sought their advice. The old couple excused themselves for a moment and entered their bedroom. When they returned, they told him what their candid feelings about the experience were.

"Women of her kind," Nana Dogo began tactfully, "exceptionally charming, are usually married spiritually. The spirits always want the best. We suggest a breakup now, but you must compensate her as best you could. Your mother and I will propitiate the spirits on your behalf."

"I think I'm convinced, Papa," Joe Boye said, looking quite relieved now. "I'll do exactly as you've suggested."

The following day, Joe Boye visited the woman and had a lengthy conversation with her. It was around the onset of evening, and she was accidentally alone in the room. Her roommates were probably gone to meet their boyfriends.

"The issue in hand is a very delicate one, Serwaa. And I think the best way to deal with it is to break up amicably. I've already informed my parents about the decision and my mind's actually made up."
"Oh Joe, so soon? Not even a second chance for me?"
"You have to understand the situation, Serwaa. It's actually a matter of life and death. But I'm ready to do anything for you as compensation. Just go ahead and mention anything you'd want me do for you."
"I want nothing but your love, Joe. It's you I want."
"I wish I could marry you, Serwaa. I just wish I could live the rest of my life with you. But you see,

my dear, our wishes are always subject to Mother Nature's approval. I'm afraid we have to accept our fate. I still insist on a breakup, but you must tell me what the compensation should be."

"Well, since your mind's made up, I guess I should let things lie. And with regard to 'the compensation', as you put it, I was wondering if you could rent a room for me. We're crowded here."

"I think that'll be better. You really need your privacy."

CHAPTER 13

An Effort to Unravel the Mystery

Shortly, Joe Boye rented a standard single room for the woman and furnished it modestly but stylishly. Then he took her to the place one afternoon, handed her the keys and kissed her goodbye for good.

Serwaa-Akoto returned home very depressed, as if someone so dear to her heart was dead. As though she did not meet anyone in the room, she sat quietly in the sofa and shed helpless tears. Her friends, surprised at, and confused about, the behaviour, could not remain incurious.

Pokuaa: "Ah, what's wrong, baby girl?"
Serwaa-Akoto: "Joe Boye just said goodbye to me for good. He took me to a room he had rented and furnished for me, handed me the keys and kissed me goodbye."

Yaa-Yaa: "Oh come off it, girlfriend, he's been fair to you at least. You should actually be grateful for how reasonably he has treated you. For me, that young man is Angel Michael. Any other man would have chased you out of his room the instant the incident occurred."

Comfort: "You just have to take consolation in what he's done for you and cheer up, baby girl."

Serwaa-Akoto: "Well, thanks for your soothing remarks, girls. But can I make a suggestion?"

The others: "Just go ahead, girlfriend. We're all ears."

Serwaa-Akoto: "Well, I don't mean any harm, first and foremost. But now that I've got a whole room all to myself, I was wondering if Yaa-Yaa would move in with me. But trust me, girls, we shall still remain as close as ever."

Yaa-Yaa: "That wasn't a bad suggestion, girlfriend. In fact, it was a brilliant one, only there's a little problem."

Comfort: "Sorry, girlfriend, but it's either all three of us move in with you or you move in alone. We're bound to stay together. In fact, we're bound to do everything together."

Pokuaa: "She's said it all, girlfriend. Doing everything together was a promise, or rather a vow we made at the very beginning of our friendship. And I'm afraid we can't break it now or ever. Only two

things may make us part company - marriage and, God forbid, death."
Serwaa-Akoto: "Mmm? Well, anyway, I guess I should let things lie. But I'll miss everyone dearly."
The others: "We'll miss you dearly too, girlfriend."

Three days later, Serwaa-Akoto moved bag and baggage to her new place in Botanso, another suburban community. It was quite far away from, and less busy than, the former.

As soon as she settled in, she made frantic efforts to penetrate the mysteries of her relationships. First, she went back to Kunso and told her parents about the mystifying sexual experience.

The couple remained dumbfounded and confused for a while. And all the while the woman was shedding uncontrollable tears, compelling her daughter to shed tears too. Being a woman and a mother, she really empathised with the poor young woman. She felt that she did not deserve to be going through such a terrible ordeal. The man too felt great sympathy for his daughter. But he behaved manly.

After some time, the couple regained their composure somewhat and made a move towards dealing with the problem.

"We're consulting the spirits first thing tomorrow morning," Papa Gyabaa said. "This mystery can't be happening to our only daughter."

"You never said a truer word, my dear," Naana Dumaa added.

The following morning, as early as possible, the family arrived in Bonkutu, the abode of Bosompem, the proverbial god, and his associates. The traditional priest who was yet to commence the day's work welcomed them and offered them a seat, a fairly long bench. Then he asked them to have patience while he carried out the preliminary activities. They were actually the first visitors to the place that day.

A while later, when the man was set, he called the family to 'the consulting room' and attended to them. They were still the only visitors there.

Priest: "The gods already know the purpose of your visit - they are all-knowing. Your daughter is destined to marry one particular man, a total stranger. And until she meets him, she can never get married."
Papa Gyabaa: "But how, Nana? I mean, how can she meet him, where and when?"
Priest: "He will come to her himself at the right time. He will be the only man who will succeed in sleeping with her and breaking her virginity for that matter."
Papa Gyabaa: "Thank you, Nana. And if you will excuse us, we must get going."
Priest: "One more thing, lovely family - it is just by way of advice. It is always prudent to make the best choices in every situation. It is equally very important

to fulfil every promise or covenant you make. Always remember one thing, that the evil people do always lives after them. You may now leave in peace."
Papa Gyabaa: "Thank you, Nana. We are very grateful indeed."
Priest: "Not at all."

Serwaa-Akoto returned to Oseikrom the following day. Now, she had conceived an interesting idea. Having had the mystery about the strange sexual experience unravelled, at least partially, her sole, desperate aim was to search for her husband. "He must find me at once," she said to herself. "Or I'll find him myself." She did not, however, rule out the fact that she was about to move mountains.

Soon, the woman had a well thought-out plan with which she hoped to find the mystery man. She decided to pretend to be born again and find a church to attend.

The plan was carried out the following Sunday. Serwaa-Akoto attended the Kwanpa Church in the neighbourhood. By sheer coincidence, the theme for the sermon that was well preached was 'Salvation', and the memory verse was Matthew 11:28. The summary of all of it was as follows: "Anyone who is weary of labour and is heavily burdened should come to Jesus Christ. He is ever ready to give the sinner peace and rest. He is ever prepared to exchange His weightless burden for the heavy one of the poor sinner."

Although she had faked repentance, the close coincidence of the sermon with her plan was to her astonishment. "Indeed, God works in mysterious ways," she felt.

During 'the call to the altar', the woman was the first person to respond. She stepped up enthusiastically and stood beside the lectern, facing the sizeable congregation. A few others who were also moved to repent and get born again joined her. The whole place reverberated with the thunderous applause that followed the bold decision. With one accord, they were made to confess their repentance as well as their acceptance of Jesus Christ as their Lord and personal Saviour. That quickly done, the pastor prayed for them and then led them to his office. There, their names were added to the list of unconfirmed members pending their baptism.

Serwaa-Akoto attended church every day, at dawn and in the evening. She also never absented herself from the new converts' class that was held on Friday afternoons. Motivated by her motive, no doubt about it, she actively and tirelessly participated in every church activity. She again ensured that she fulfilled every financial obligation.

Soon, she caught the attention of the entire congregation. But she was yet to be baptised and confirmed. As time went by, she became conversant with every church activity as well as familiar with virtually every member of the church. And no sooner had she been considered versed in the doctrine and activities of the church than she was recommended for the sacraments.

Now, the young woman was a full member of the growing church and one of the lead singers. She had a unique, silky voice that made her sing like an angel. No one could resist her angelic voice anytime she held the microphone. Everyone would be on their feet and in their best mood whenever the adorable woman led praises. And whenever she led worship, oh my God, the Holy Spirit actually descended in His full glory to fill everyone!

Every member of the community church expressively admired the woman who simply personified holiness despite her incomparable beauty and charm. They especially cherished her growing passion for Christ. Unfortunately, the presence of the Holy Spirit in her was yet to be made manifest. Baptism by the Holy Spirit was the main measure of one's holiness and level of maturity among the Pentecostal fraternity. And the speaking in tongues, for them, was the only manifestation of it.

The 'dedicated' Christian prayed, fasted and tried all other means for receiving the spiritual gift in vain. She was getting desperate, for most of the members with whom she got confirmed now spoke in tongues. "I must speak in tongues too," she felt, "either by hook or by crook."

At one special vigil, the young woman was compelled to feign receipt of the Holy Spirit after all the frantic efforts had failed to produce results. She suddenly began to speak in tongues after a touch on her forehead by the pastor. Pre-rehearsed perhaps, she actually spoke intensely in the strange tongues and made an impression on everyone. But it neither appeared strange nor surprising, for her passion for Christ and commitment to church activities clearly justified it. Everybody felt that the special gift was even long overdue.

The young woman's fake baptism by the Holy Spirit went a long way towards affirming her spiritual growth in the sight of the congregation. She was now rated as widely ahead of all her fellow young women in terms of spiritual growth and dedication. And in terms of beauty, charm and grace, she was without equal. In fact, she never ceased to amaze the congregation.

Soon, the Holy Spirit began to speak to the young men about Serwaa-Akoto. Most of them, leaders and ordinary members alike, began to have dreams and visions about her. Interestingly, each of them claimed the Holy Spirit had revealed the young woman as their better half.

In the midst of the avalanche of false revelations about her, the beauty incarnate was bombarded with marriage proposals. But since she had a mental picture of the man she was destined to get married to she did not make any silly mistakes. She tactfully turned down each of them without hesitation. Desperate though, she knew which side her bread was buttered and did not allow just any man to manoeuvre himself into her life.

The much sought-after wife material remained selective until she finally met her heart's desire. One night, right after church, the first son of the pastor proposed to her right under the church's giant sign-post. Oh what a dream come true! Having fallen for the good-looking young man since she joined the church, Serwaa-Akoto was all smiles. She accepted the proposal virtually instantly.

The announcement of their courtship, the Christian way, of course, followed shortly. Interestingly, it marked the end of the work of the Holy Spirit in the single young men. None of them had any vision or revelation about her again. The young couple who were widely described as a perfect pair courted for only a short while and got married. They had a memorable wedding that attracted record attendance. Sadly, the woman did not invite her friends, her former roommates, perhaps for personal reasons.

The newly married couple lived alone in a three-bed-room house that shared a wall with 'the mission house' in which the man's family lived. Although the union typified a Christian marriage and was thus exemplary, it was heavily laden with problems. The son of the man of God too never succeeded in making love to his wedded wife. As usual, the fully potent young man would lose erection at the point of insertion.

The unfortunate young husband decided to be more mature in his reaction and thus kept silent about the ordeal. He felt that it was too embarrassing a problem to share. Besides, he felt it was too early to share his marital problems. He did not even confide in his own parents.

But the teaser was, for how long could he endure the 'sexual hunger'?

By the way, the young couple continued to fast and pray and hoped to surmount the problem sooner or later. But it appeared that the peculiar marital problem was beyond their capabilities. The ceaseless prayers and periodic 'dry' fasts seemed less potent a solution to the serious problem. Eventually, the young man became frustrated. Now, he felt he had no option but to break his silence.

One evening, he summoned up courage and broke the news to his parents. Pastor and Mrs. Opuni were taken aback by what their son had managed to endure since he got married. They, however, pleaded with him to exercise more patience while they intervened diplomatically.

Unfortunately, the concerted efforts of the concerned parents and the young couple could not deal with the problem. Eventually, the devastated couple were left hanging. But, obviously, the young man was running out of patience.

The sad failure of the next exercise was the final straw. Directed by the Holy Spirit, according to the woman, the couple embarked upon a two-week 'dry' fasting and prayer. But the undertaking was without much conviction on the man's part. For him, it was nothing if not a boring repetition of the same old course of action.

Not surprisingly, the marathon exercise proved fruitless. The 'starving' husband was still unsuccessful in the several attempts he made to make love to his wife afterwards. Then one night, after he had failed again, he suddenly lost his temper and began to rant and rave. "This marriage isn't worth a damn!" he roared. Then he went ahead and threatened divorce, bringing the 'for better or for worse' marriage vow into disrepute.

After the fateful night, the marriage gradually fell on the rocks and could never be salvaged. Although the revered pastor and his wife as well as other respected leaders of the church intervened, they only made a vain effort. Sampene Opuni was no longer interested in 'the utter hell of a marriage', as he put it. Eventually, the young marriage had to be dissolved. But the dissolution had to be disguised as separation in order to preserve the integrity of the pastor as well as the church.

CHAPTER 14

Serwaa-Akoto Prostitutes Herself

Now, the virgin divorcée had to move out of Sampene's house. Clearly, they had no business staying together again. Some quick arrangements were made for her immediate relocation to Sabaaba, another distant suburb of the city.

Sadly, the divorce and subsequent relocation of the divorcée marked the end of her membership of the community church. It even ended her membership of the Christendom in general. The actual reason for calling it quits remained unknown. But she may have realised that the plan for finding her true husband did not have to remain static.

Gradually, Serwaa-Akoto managed to overcome the trauma of the divorce. Now, she looked as dynamic as ever. Strangely enough, she did not give up the fight. She was still determined to find the particular man she was destined to get married to. She even appeared more desperate now than ever before and did not seem to care about the means. 'The end justifies the means' was very probably the new philosophy.

In any case, the second plan ought to be effective. It had to be clever enough to enable her find the particular man as early as possible. Age was gradually catching up with her and thus her beauty and charm were gradually diminishing.

After days of painstaking consideration and reconsideration of alternatives, however, the decision she finally made was outrageous. The woman who was desperate to find her true husband resolved to prostitute herself. Absolutely sickening! By the way, she claimed to have two reasons for the shocker. Although her priority remained finding the special man of a husband, she felt that she could make a living as well. The woman was quite convinced that she could find the special man from the numerous men who would pay for her sexual services. At the same time, she felt, she would be earning some income to maintain herself.

True to her word, Serwaa-Akoto joined a bevy of prostitutes who operated around Hotel De Paradise. But she always disguised herself at work, just like most of her colleagues. They paraded along the Konkonsa Road every night. It was a very busy road beside which the hotel was located. They would put on skimpy and revealing skirts and dresses and flaunt themselves to seduce passersby, including patrons of the hotel.

As usual, Serwaa-Akoto, now Shena, was the most preferred prostitute by virtue of her striking beauty and charm. She had too many customers to attend to every night. By a rough estimate, at least twenty men, including unscrupulous husbands with insatiable drive for sex, took her away and, or to the hotel in a night. But none of them would succeed in sleeping with her. As usual, each one of them would strangely lose erection while attempting insertion. And out of fear or shame or both, they would pay up and ask her to leave.

The eerie experience kept happening to, embarrassing and, or alarming every customer every night. And only a handful of them still ignored the popular adage, 'Once bitten twice shy', and made another attempt. But none of them was too foolish to ever make a third attempt. So little by little, the virgin prostitute lost each customer one after the other.

Eventually, Shena Baby, as everyone fondly called her, became the Cinderella among her colleagues. Virtually no man requested for her services again and that began to tell on her living. Her colleagues found the turn of events astounding. The vast majority were quick to speculate that she definitely had a secret with which she attracted the numerous customers she used to have. They felt that she certainly had a magic portion or a charm of some sort. And they concluded quite convincingly that her luck had suddenly run out because the particular juju had finally lost its potency.

Closely connected with the nocturnal trade was smoking. It was virtually a tradition. Every prostitute was a potential smoker and Shena Baby was without exception. She had long taken to the habit and now she really enjoyed it. She also drank quite heavily. Her indulgence in the habits was getting a little excessive at present. It was gradually becoming an addiction. Her threatened livelihood may have accounted for that.

It had been ages since Serwaa-Akoto last heard from, called or visited the inseparable trio. Now, she seemed to have detached herself from them and vice versa. Her relocation had virtually severed the close relationship she once had with them, especially Yaa-Yaa.

One afternoon, she chanced on Pokuaa at the supermarket and their emotional reactions virtually caused a scene. But for the security guard's timely signal, the two would have messed about. They were too delighted as well as surprised to bump into each other.

After they had exchanged some rather lengthy pleasantries, they went ahead and shared some surprises. Now, they were outside the supermarket and were virtually alone.

Pokuaa started the ball rolling. She said that the other girls were now happily married. She quickly added that she was getting married too in a week's time. Serwaa-Akoto could not help cheering. She was full of happiness for her old friends. And she kept glowing with the emotion throughout the conversation. In the midst of the seemingly endless chat, the would-be wife seized the opportunity to invite her old friend to the pending wedding.

Blissfully unaware, Serwaa-Akoto was only pretending. She had only managed to stay composed and glow with joy in order to please her friend. Deep down, she was hopelessly jealous. She felt that fate had not been fair to her. Now, she probably had to try harder since the feeling was heightening, or her friend would become suspicious.

"I'm really happy for you and I wish you well, girl-friend," she said in pretended cheer. "But you must remember me in prayer so my luck will change too. And do expect me on the big day. I can hardly wait to be there."

"By the way," she added, "I'm now a waitress at Hotel De Paradise. So you may pass through one day and say hi."

"Oh that's great news, girlfriend!" she remarked cheerfully. "That place is heaven on earth! You're always a lucky girl, girlfriend."

But, obviously, that was a very big lie, the reason for which was best known to her. However, creating the impression that she was gainfully employed now could be a wild guess.

Serwaa-Akoto locked herself away in her room and wept bitterly with jealousy when she got home. Occasionally, she paused and sipped some 'Alomo' Bitters. She actually had a full bottle of the chilled herbal drink beside her. Then she would make some sarcastic comments about the old friends' good fortune.

While she kept crying, drinking to excess and muttering to herself, Shena Baby made the following interesting remarks one moment: "If no Adam is interested in this elegance, maybe alcohol does. And as for that girl's pending wedding, I won't even dare. I just can't have the courage to be there. Oh no, I can't. It'll be another fertile ground for humiliation."

Poor Serwaa-Akoto went on crying, drinking and smoking until she was roaring drunk. Eventually, she slept her distress away and never woke up until nightfall.

Now, it was time again to go to work, and as usual, she began to wonder if her luck would ever change. She was already torn apart by the worsening prospects of the job and its effects on her living. The tension heightened as she hesitantly got prepared. Then, when she was set, she stalked off slowly and gloomily to the roadside. Finally, she boarded a car to the workplace to try her luck again.

Unfortunately, luck was not on her side yet. For nearly three hours or so, no single man approached the woman who was once the men's baby, adding to her misery. She remained confused and disturbed by the bad luck until she began to contemplate closing work prematurely. But just before the thought could be finalised, a man in late middle age, the only stranger in Jerusalem, got off his car and walked straight to her. He was tall and dark-complexioned, and he was in an expensive smock. He had a peculiar smell. The particular perfume he had on was too strong to be pleasant. In fact, it was a bit of a nuisance.

"Would you mind sleeping over, young lady?"
"No, Sir, not at all."

At once, they walked to the car, got into it and away it zoomed. Shena Baby was still smoking and at the same time chewing a gum noisily. Occasionally, she stared at the man, smiled and puffed out a cloud of smoke delight-edly. A while later, the man, seemingly uncomfortable with the smoking in particular, engaged her in a brief conversation.

"Would you mind putting out the cigarette, young woman?"
"Oh no, not at all, Sir. Your wish's actually my command."
"Thanks. You know, I used to enjoy smoking when I was much younger, but not anymore. I was actually advised by my doctor to put a stop to the habit or I'd shorten my life."
"Oh really? Then I guess I must put a stop to it at once."
"You never said a truer word, my dear."
"Thanks for the piece of advice, Sir."
"That's all right."

Shena Baby and the man finally reached their destination, an isolated place on the outskirts of the city. It was entirely new to the woman. They entered a house, a mansion of some sort which was as quiet as the cemetery. A wave of alarm suddenly engulfed the woman and aroused her curiosity.

"Emm, do you live here alone, Sir?"
"Oh no, there're other occupants. I actually live here with my siblings and many others."
"Never mind, I asked because the house is too quiet."
"Oh really? Well, just now they must all be asleep. And I don't think they'll tolerate any disturbance."
"OK."

The foreplay began as soon as they entered the bedroom, and by and by both of them were in the mood. But Shena Baby definitely knew that the arousal was only bound to be a nine-day wonder. To her amazement as well as delight, however, a chequered history was made. The jinx was overcome! The mysterious ageing man succeeded in making the old virgin lose her virginity that night.

The woman simultaneously remained astounded and delighted for some time. Her expressive face and other mannerisms said it all. Then suddenly, she remembered what the fetish priest said during the brief consultation and nearly screamed in disappointment. "This is really unbelievable!" she strained to mutter to herself. "This old man, of all men?" She simply found it hard to believe that she was actually destined to marry a man who was even older than her father. In fact, she felt hard done by Mother Nature.

Suddenly, she ceased to be responsive. She stayed aloof throughout the rest of the act. Of course, she remained perplexed and distressed too.

The man slept with the woman just once and fell into a deep sleep afterwards. Then the woman, preoccupied with dismay, lay awake for a while and eventually got hypnotised. Shortly, she saw herself fast asleep and dreaming. The deep sleep was full of terrible nightmares about deaths, burial processions, graves and ghosts.

Shena Baby virtually fainted when she woke up the following morning. Having slept in, she was suddenly aroused by the cawing crows, only to discover the shock of her life. Incredibly, she was lying alone on a tomb in a cemetery. "Christ!" she yelled at the top of her voice, trembling instantly with terrible fright. Her whole body was now shrouded in goose pimples. Then, not knowing the direction she should go, she finally found her way to the roadside, and not a moment too soon.

Restless, sobbing and scared to death, she tried to stop every passing car without regard to its destination. All she wished for now was to be rescued. But it seemed that the wish would not come true anytime soon. Only a few cars plied the short feeder and thus they were quite difficult to come by.

At last, a taxi that had a vacant seat picked her to the next town. Fairly relieved now, she approached a driver who gave her directions back to the city.

CHAPTER 15

Serwaa-Akoto Turns Over a New Leaf

Serwaa-Akoto was so disturbed by the nightmarish experience that she wished she could share it and ease the tension. But she was prevented by fear of being disrespected or mocked because of the stigma that was attached to her job. She remained at a crossroads for a while before she finalised to keep it to herself. But she learnt her lesson. The terrifying experience marked a turning point in how the woman made a living. After a period of reflection, she turned over a new leaf and relocated to the inner city.

Now, she had to find another way of making a living. And the particular alternative had to be lucrative, at least like the one she had just given up. Having acquired expensive tastes somewhat, she certainly never envisaged going into any venture that would render her poorer.

"I think drug peddling is profitable," the reformed prostitute said in a brainstorm one moment, "more profitable even than illegal gold mining or 'galamsey'."

"But that isn't different from what I've just quit," she countered immediately. "Well, we'll see."

The woman only tried her utmost in the vain hope of getting over the trauma of the shocking experience. The vivid memories of it never ceased to be triggered. They kept haunting her day in, day out. Sometimes, she had terrible nightmares about it. At other times, she fell into trances while preoccupied with its helpless memories. The poor woman was actually being tormented.

However hard she tried, Serwaa-Akoto was still getting increasingly desperate every passing moment. Now, she felt that something needed to be done to save the situation. One moment she was struck by a thought which she decided to put into action. Shortly, she set out to consult a traditional priest about the problem. The veteran priest of Suman, the mysterious god in Pampam, was a revered man. According to the acquaintance who recommended him to the woman, he was second to none.

"Remove your footwear at once and tread cautiously, young woman. You are in the dwelling of a great god, a holy ground."
"OK, Nana. Thank you, and good day."
"Good day, innocent young woman. You are welcome."

"Thank you, Nana."

"The great god I serve is omniscient - he knows why you are here. You slept with a spirit, but you will not die. Suman the Great will be merciful."

"Oh thank you, Nana. Now, there is light at the end of the tunnel."

"You will undergo spiritual purification for three days and then fortification for three more days. And afterwards, no man other than the one who is destined to be your husband can sleep with you again. But you have the option to return and then return at your convenience for the rites."

"I am not going back with my bad luck, Nana. I am ready now."

After the six-day rites, the woman was declared completely free from any visitation. Oh what a merciful relief! She quickly expressed gratitude and made the little obligatory payment. She even added extra as a token of her thanks. Then she returned to the city a happy woman.

Shortly, the issue about livelihood was settled. The woman finally decided to run a bar and set out on it almost immediately. She rented a very big stall out of her savings and found the right people to get it ready. But afterwards, she realised she could not raise all the capital single-handedly. She soon settled on seeking the assistance of her parents. Meanwhile, she had made the necessary arrangement with some enterprises for the supply of the drinks and others.

A few weeks later, the quite promising venture was finally launched out. It was such a spacious and grand bar. Everyone was sure to admire it. The visionary woman sold assorted alcoholic and non-alcoholic drinks and cigarettes. She also sold kebab and 'mpusu' or fresh meat soup. But the former was prepared and sold separately by a veteran, a young man from the north with whom she had an agreement.

The new business that was mainly nocturnal, just like the former, boomed within a very short time. The woman may have used her dwindling beauty and charm to good effect. The central location of the place as well as its grand and lively appearance and other charms could also be the attraction.

In line with the steadily high patronage, the woman made a huge profit every week. No doubt about it, she now had the makings of a successful businesswoman. Although she did not plough back completely, she consistently invested a reasonable proportion of the profit back into the business. She also ensured that she spent wisely, living comfortably but modestly. Her top priority always remained ensuring that the business flourished. And by virtue of hard work and dynamism, it was actually booming. Serwaa-Akoto was such an ambitious woman.

The business thrived a few years later courtesy of her diligence and ingenuity. Now, Auntie Serwaa, as her cherished customers and everyone else affection-ately called her, was a rich woman. Not surprisingly, the new status had strongly influenced her lifestyle. The woman now had expensive tastes. Of course, she was more sophisticated and trendy now. The thriving business had again given her a huge sense of achievement. The pleasing emotion had really soothed her and helped her overcome most of her worries. No wonder she looked more rejuvenated and livelier now.

As time went by, she felt that there was some mis-match between her status and her home, a two-bedroom flat. She soon arranged for a more spacious four-bedroom flat in the same neighbourhood and furnished it to taste. She also provided additional security fixtures to guarantee her safety and moved in at once.

Now, most people felt the woman must be quite content. After all, she was swimming in luxury. She bought the best of things for herself, anything she found necessary or likely to add to her comfort and status. She wore the finest clothes and jewellery, ate sumptuous meals and drove a posh car. She also had the best of fun. Entertainment, any form of it, was a regular pursuit now.

But little did anyone know she was not at peace. Behind the luxury and admiration was the need for a romantic relationship at least. Although she had remained optimistic since she consulted the priest of Suman, she felt she could be deceiving herself. Not a single man had even approached her about ordinary friendship since, let alone proposed to her. The weird experience had remained a constant thorn in her flesh. It even made her feel worthless most times, especially when she could realise she was gradually passing her reproductive years.

Even the records that were played at the bar got her offended most times. The vast majority made at least a passing reference to her single and childless circumstance and thus got her humiliated. Sadly, she could not forbid their playing. Most of them tended to be the custom-ers' favourites and thus they were constantly requested. Besides, playing such records in bars was the order of the day.

Some mischievous customers too would occasionally make some derogatory remarks about the problem. Of course, everyone wondered why she was still single and childless at her age in spite of her elegance and riches. Those moments usually made the poor woman feel sorry for herself.

There was one nice man Auntie Serwaa had secretly admired for a while and virtually fallen for. Oyibo, a perfect gentleman, was one of her regular customers. He was good-looking and graceful, and he had admirable temperance. Unfortunately, the secret admirer had found it difficult attracting his attention. She did not know how best she could communicate her feelings without creating any ill impression. But one lucky afternoon, the opportunity presented itself. The two happened to be alone at the bar for quite a while. And after a period of wrestle with her emotions, the woman decided to seize the chance.

"But why are you always calm and lonely, Oyibo?"
"Well, that's what I am, actually. I'm single and lonely."
"Oh really? Then we may share a lot in common. I'm single too."
"Single with all your elegance and riches? You must be waiting for Angel Michael to marry you then?"
"Ha-ha-ha! Angel Michael? Oh no, my dear. I'm just waiting for the brave man, I mean the real man."
"Well, talk about the brave man - I'm simply daring."
"Oh really? Then you must begin to prove it, for I don't really see that quality in you."
"Mmm?"
"Oh yeah."

Having been dared, the man who was gradually getting drunk on Herb Afrik stole a kiss. But the woman showed no indifference to the act. He tried it again and again, playfully and cunningly, and now she was expressively interested. And from that moment forward, the two took an interest in each other. By and by, they made up their minds and had a relationship.

Auntie Serwaa was madly in love with the man. She was actually infatuated with him. But she had good cause to be. Desperate to get married, she felt that she could not fail to grab such a golden opportunity. But the main reason, a very big surprise, was that the lovers could do anything that a romantic relationship involved, including lovemaking. Thus, the woman was absolutely sure they were destined to marry each other. Little wonder she was determined to do anything, even the seemingly impossible, to keep him.

By the way, there was something about the relationship that really bothered the woman. Everything had been happening at her place ever since they met. They had actually been cohabiting in her flat. The man had never taken her to his house before and that had remained a real bother. Quite apart from that, he had never told her anything about his background. But he knew everything about her.

Sometimes, she was even tempted to believe that he was probably a fugitive. But she would quickly counter the illusion on the basis of the gentleman's personality. She felt that he was too gentle a man to be entangled in any illegality.

Auntie Serwaa frequently impressed on the man the need to open up to her. She felt that knowing something about his background, however little it may be, would make her understand and appreciate him better. Sadly, everything always fell on deaf ears. Oyibo always remained unforthcoming.

"But how can I cohabit with, and ultimately get married to, a man I know nothing about?" she said to herself one moment. "How'd I even introduce him to my parents and others? All I know about him is Oyibo, and only God knows whether that's even his real name."

The poor woman wished she could pressure the man into telling her more about himself as well as taking her home. But she was mindful that she may end up losing him if her actions were misconstrued. But little by little, she kept putting some weak pressure on him to take her home especially. At some point she mustered courage, intensified the pressure and remained insistent. Now, she even threatened a breakup sometimes. But no doubt that was only a pretence. Having proven beyond doubt that he was her God-given husband, she was ready to move heaven and earth to keep him. The only source of the little courage she had was the realisation that the man was madly in love too. But, as usual, he remained unflappable and adamant.

Despite her fears, the woman in love tactfully persisted with the mild pressure until the man finally yielded on one condition. Auntie Serwaa had to promise her unshaken love for him first. Explaining himself, Oyibo said he had a premonition that the relationship would sever after taking her home. He added quite pitifully that his strange background was likely to disappoint her expectations and cause a breakup. The woman who was ready to do anything to keep the relationship obliged without hesitation and allayed his fears. Afterwards, they had a deal.

Oyibo agreed to take the woman home on the coming Saturday. By implication, the all-important visit was only three days away. Although it was not part of the deal, the virtuous woman tried to impress on the man the prudence in spending at least a night at the place. And even though he nodded in agreement, it was obvious it lacked conviction.

CHAPTER 16

A Night at Her Would-be Husband's House

At long last, it was Saturday. The rising sun was bright and thus the morning was clear. Auntie Serwaa was all smiles. She glowed with excitement every passing moment. She sang all day and occasionally danced rather spontaneously. The woman again daydreamt time and again and even forgot her routine. She was really expectant. But something nearly wiped the smile off her face.

It was almost midday now, but the man was yet to say something about the planned visit. A while later, when she still hadn't heard anything from him, it struck her to remind him about it.

"I hope you haven't forgotten about the visit, my dear?" she said sweetly and cheerfully.

"Don't worry, dear," he replied softly, "the day's still young. At least let me enjoy the best part of it first." The man's response was as clear as mud.

The hours went by so fast, but all the while the man remained silent about the visit. Now, the sun was fast setting and the woman was gradually getting busy at the bar. But she was still eager to hear something from the man. Sadly, he still seemed unconcerned with the deal. It even appeared as though he had had a change of mind. He kept his distance and tried to keep himself busy with any unnecessary thing. Realising his indifference, the woman decided to remind him about it again.

"I do hope we're setting out any moment from how, my dear?"

"Just give me a little more time, dear. I'll soon get set."

"Well, if you don't mind my saying so, it's getting late and I'm gradually getting busy. The night promises to be very busy, you know."

"Well, you'll have to make a choice, dear."

Weekend nights were her busiest moments and that particular Saturday night was without exception. Although she was only too eager to be at the man's place, she also felt bound to satisfy her numerous customers first. Most of them actually preferred her services to those of the waitresses. And no doubt they would complain bitterly about her absence on such a busy night.

Hours later, she eventually became less busy and entrusted the care of the bar to the waitresses. It was about half past nine now.

"I know it's late, dear, but we still have to go."
"Not a problem, dear. Your wish's my command."
"You're a darling, dear. But if you don't mind, I'd charter a taxi to drop us off? I don't drive well at night, you know."
"No, I don't, dear. But don't bother, I've already called a friend of mine, a taxi driver, to drop us off."
"How proactive my darling has been! Here, a very special kiss for my darling."

Shortly, the taxi, virtually brand new, arrived. They quickly got in and drove off. They drove through known streets and suburbs of the Garden City to entirely new and desolate places.

"I never knew the place was too far, my dear."
"Well, I'm really sorry, dear, but that was one of the reasons why I was quite reluctant to take you there. But worry no more, for we're almost there."
"That's all right, dear."

At last, they arrived at the place, a well-lit city in a valley. It was as beautiful as the Garden of Eden. But it was too lonely. They drove past the city centre and finally parked in front of a magnificent mansion. Then the lovers got off and entered the house while the driver waited in the car. It was very quiet inside.

"Do other people live here, my dear?"
"Of course yes, a whole lot of them, actually. But how could just an individual live in this big mansion all alone, my dear?"
"But I can't find anyone around, my dear."
"Oh, Auntie Serwaa! Isn't it too late to find anyone around? They must all be asleep and wouldn't want to be disturbed."
"Well, if you say so."

Auntie Serwaa was still unconvinced of the man's claims. She especially had doubts as to whether the place was actually his home. She was again doubtful whether other people lived there since there was no sure indication. While she kept wondering, she suddenly had an idea.

"I was wondering if we could ask the driver to leave so we could spend the night here, my dear. I really need to meet your family as well as familiarise myself with the place."

"But this is certainly not our last visit, my dear. I think we should return and come back another time since we didn't plan to spend the night."

"Oh no, dear. This is our second home and we don't need to plan specially before spending a night here. I insist we do, please. Let's go and ask him to go."

Against his wish, obviously, the man straggled behind the woman as they headed towards the entrance. To her utter surprise when they opened the gate, both the driver and the car were nowhere to be found. They had actually vanished from the face of the earth.

"Ah, my dear," the woman said in complete bewilderment, "how come we didn't hear anything about the car zooming off? The whole city is so still that we should have even heard the humming of the engine however new it might be."

"Well, dear," Oyibo remarked innocently, "puzzling though, I think there's no need worrying about it. After all, we don't owe him, and he doesn't owe us either."

On that pre-emptive note, they returned to the house and ceased to communicate for a while. Auntie Serwaa sat in stunned silence in a single sofa. She was still trying to sort out the mystery. But the man was incurious. Apparently, he was unhappy about the woman's growing curiosity.

Minutes later, they settled down and began to require each other's attentions. The woman suddenly joined the man in the longest sofa and gave him a peck on the cheek. Then, little by little, the fondling, cuddling and kissing put them in the mood for lovemaking. When the mood finally took them, they had it smoothly. But Sleep, the cunning abductor, suddenly cut the romantic moment short. As usual, he sneaked into the bedroom, drugged the lovers and then took them away.

Sadly, the woman was soon landed in the trickster's hell where she had a deep but bad sleep. She had episodes of terrible nightmares that scared the life out of her.

The following morning, she shockingly found herself in a cemetery once again. She suddenly woke up to discover in disbelief that she was lying alone on a tomb. Initially, she was petrified. But she quickly realised it was a second-time experience and calmed down somewhat. Then she realised again that she was at the same cemetery she found herself the other time. Now, astonishment suddenly took over from fright. But the tenure of the new boss was short-lived. He was soon replaced by confusion when the woman learnt that she was lying on the same tomb on which she lay the other time.

Then, spontaneously, she fled to the roadside, guessed the direction right and boarded a passing car to the nearest town. From there, she found her way back to the city.

"I can no longer keep this to myself," she said to herself. "Oh no, I can't. It may even have some dire consequences on me." She was still on a minibus en route to Oseikrom.

As soon as she got home, she plucked up courage and told everyone about the mystery. The bold disclosure triggered considerable sympathy for the poor woman. The women especially empathised with her strongly. "You'll have to seek spiritual protection to avoid another visitation," most of them advised. It again had a great therapeutic effect. It helped to alleviate the trauma, fear and despair that had engulfed her.

Although she had managed to calm down, the poor woman still required an explanation for the horrifying experience. She simply couldn't decipher why ghosts alone succeeded in sleeping with her. One moment while she was wondering, she suddenly remembered something: "You will undergo spiritual purification for three days and then fortification for three more days. And afterwards, no man other than the one who is destined to be your husband can sleep with you again."

"Ah," she wondered, "wasn't that the old priest's assurance? Or he just deceived me?"

A few days later, she went on a follow-up visit to Pampam, the dwelling of Suman, the supposed great god. She was desperate for an explanation for the fathomless situation. Familiar with the rules, she removed her footwear even before she got to the entrance. Then she trod cautiously on the supposed holy ground until she reached where the queue to 'the consulting room' had been formed. As usual, the human train was quite long and discouraging. But she did not have an alternative.

She only pulled a face and joined it, her impatience clearly noticeable.

Hours later, when it was almost dusky, it eventually got to her turn. But just before she was called in, the priest had a strange visitor. A male spirit, a humanoid, materialised there. He was awful and frightening, and he appeared more powerful. Suddenly, and in a roaring voice, he gave the man a stern warning against any attempt at helping the woman.

"You must not even welcome her here - now or ever!" he said. "Or you will be entangled in a never-ending war."

"Your wish is my command, Mighty One," the frail priest replied humbly. Satisfied with the response, the spirit disappeared at once.

"Call the next person in, Asubor," he ordered the attendant at the top of his voice. As usual, the young man was standing at the door waiting for an order. Blissfully unaware, Auntie Serwaa went in and stood before the old priest who was now as restless as a wild dog. Before she could even open her mouth to greet him, he roared suddenly.

> "You are evil, woman! And hence the great god does not want to have anything to do with you again! As a matter of fact, your next appearance here will be considered a trespass! Just leave with your troubles now!"

"Ah, but what did I do to deserve all this humiliation, Nana?"

"What an impudent woman! So you still have the guts to talk back to me? You'd best leave my presence now, or I'll make you suffer the worst of misfortunes!"

Having scared the life out of her, Auntie Serwaa fled the place like a jet. Now, she was more burdened with trauma and perplexity than ever. She felt that the man had first and foremost lied to her and, as if that was not bad enough, gone ahead to rub salt in a wound. The unfounded accusation he made against her was what she even found most puzzling. Altogether, she felt cheated by the old priest.

Auntie Serwaa remained preoccupied with distress when she finally got home. She managed to have a bath and then locked up. Then she went to bed on an empty stomach in the hope of sleeping her worries away.

Sadly, she only made a vain effort at forcing herself to sleep. However hard she tried, the helpless thoughts would not let her succeed. She even tried the power of music in vain. The poor woman was so deep in thought that she was completely oblivious to the soothing melodies, her favourites. She eventually had to take some sleeping tablets before she could sleep her troubles away.

Quite interestingly, the poor woman did not give up the ghost. She felt that the time to throw in the towel was not yet. She was very tenacious indeed. "I still have to get out of this predicament," she muttered to herself one moment. "I'm not a spirit and thus I can't have anything to do with spirits. My real husband must find me, or I must find him."

Some weeks later, she went back to the village and told the family about the eerie experiences.

> Naana Dumaa: "I suggest we visit Bonkutu first thing tomorrow morning."
> Serwaa-Akoto: "Exactly why I'm here, Maame."
> Papa Gyabaa: "I think we don't have an alternative. We should all get ready to set out at dawn."

The next morning, before daybreak, the family set off to Bonkutu and arrived before sunrise. As usual, the proverbial, veteran priest was already at work. But the only visitor they met there was a woman who had just been attended to. Unknown to them, however, the ageing priest had got a strange visitor in 'the consulting room'. The mystery male spirit was simply awkward.

> "Make no attempt to help the family that will be in next, and don't dare to disobey me!"
> "No one teaches me how to do my job, except the gods I serve."
> "And what do they say in regard to your next visitors?"

"The poor woman cannot continue to pay the price for what she knows nothing about."

"But the harm is already done and is irrevocable."

"No request can be granted unless it is ordained by the gods."

"I can infer you are just stubborn. You will lose your voice as soon as you lay eyes on them. And you will remain dumb until you have a change of mind."

In the midst of the heated exchange, the attendant knocked on the door. He was leading the visitors in. Instantly, the spirit disappeared.

"Mmm! Mmm! Mmm!" the fetish priest mimed as soon as he set eyes on the family. And that meant, "Go away!"

At once, the young man drove them away, following them as far as to the main entrance. Then he gave them a stern warning against coming back again.

Astonished, baffled and embarrassed, the family made the return journey on empty stomachs. They resolved to keep everything to themselves and think about the next course of action. But later, the concerned parents felt it was better to let sleeping dogs lie. No doubt about it, they only sounded cruel to be kind. They had definitely learnt a lesson from the bitter experience which was a repeat of what their daughter had earlier suffered at the temple of Suman. After all, the saying goes, 'Once bitten twice shy'. So they certainly meant well.

Accordingly, and with tact and diplomacy, they advised the woman to accept her fate, however appalling it was, and learn to live with it. And even though she believed that all hope was not lost yet, she felt bound to listen to her parents. Deep down, she felt she could not remain single and childless for the rest of her life. Apparently, she was not utterly despaired yet.

CHAPTER 17

Serwaa-Akoto Disowns Her Family

Now, the woman was very depressed about her plight. She felt that she was too innocent to go through such an ordeal. One moment she blamed Mother Nature for her injustice. She felt that the old woman had been too cruel to her. But she equally felt that the family could never be blameless.

"Enmity, just like charity, begins at home," she felt. "And if there are no enemies from within, those from outside cannot be so immovably cruel." At once, she began to turn against the family. She strongly felt that her parents especially could be her secret enemies. "They wouldn't suggest I lived with humiliation forever if they knew nothing about the problem," she thought.

A few days later, she went down to the village again. She was boiling with rage to confront her parents to enquire into whatever they knew about her predicament.

She was actually consumed by the emotion and she seemed unstoppable.

Serwaa-Akoto: "You must tell me everything the two of you know about my predicament. And you'd better go ahead now before I do anything silly."
Naana Dumaa: "You must be out of your mind, Serwaa-Akoto! You're talking to your parents, for Christ's sake!"
Serwaa-Akoto: "You'd better stop the pretence and tell it all, Maame. I'm beginning to run out of patience."
Papa Gyabaa: "What are you insinuating, young woman? Are you now suspecting us, your own parents, of having a hand in your predicament? Something that all of us are worried about? No, dear, you must apologise to us at once, for you just called me a wizard and your mother a witch by inference."
Naana Dumaa: "Exactly! You must go down on your knees and apologise now, first to your father and then to me."
Serwaa-Akoto: "I'll do nothing of that sort, Maame! I'll even carry it to extremes if you don't admit having a part to play in my ordeal now!"

On that horrifying note, the poor couple burst out shedding helpless tears. They really found it hard to believe their only daughter's baseless accusations. They remained speechless with disbelief as she went on ranting and raving. And as if that was not bad enough, she finished off by disowning the family in its entirety. She even went as far as to describe the village as accursed as well as swear that she would never set foot there again.

Although they were terribly hurt by the extent of the misbehaviour, the loving parents managed to bite their tongues. Knowing that two wrongs would never make a right, they did not utter a word against her. Instead, they managed to tolerate her throughout. They ensured that the great love and affection they had for her remained intact. When she was finally gone, they talked briefly about it and then brushed everything aside.

"But what at all came over our daughter, Papa Gyabaa? How in heaven's name could a daughter treat her own parents with such disrespect?"
"I don't think I can guess any imaginable grounds for such misbehaviour, my dear. Perhaps it was frustration - frustration at not having a husband yet."
"Well, I should think so, my lord. Oh Mother Nature, please be merciful to our only daughter and grant her heart's desire!"
"You never said a truer word, Maame Dumaa. But I think you should have besought the old woman's mercy upon the entire family. After all, our daughter's burning desire is the whole family's burning desire too."

"You're perfectly right, my lord. Please, Mother Nature, be merciful to us and grant us our hearts' desire!"
"That was better, my dear."

After months of sleeplessness and growing unease, Auntie Serwaa finally came to terms with her ordeal. Having realised that life was more precious than marriage and children, she finally resolved to content herself with her life and her success. Now, her business, the goose that laid the golden eggs, became her husband, her family and everything. She also made Oseikrom, the Garden City, her home.

The poor single worked diligently day and night to see the business grow. Ambitious to maximise the fortunes of the business, she smartly opened branches in other busy places. Now, Obaa Pa Spot was gradually becoming a household name in the whole big city. Soon, the new branches boomed and Auntie Serwaa and luxury were bedfellows now. The confirmed single acquired all the luxurious things in the world.

Not surprisingly, Auntie Serwaa felt that her accommodation was no longer luxurious. She was particularly discontented with the location which she now found unadventurous. So she made the necessary arrangements and before long took up residence in Sikaman. The place was one of the most expensive residential suburbs of the city.

Auntie Serwaa still lived alone in a four-bedroom flat. But, as usual, she had a casual housekeeper who never slept over. Proactive, she had already acquired four plots of land and started a house, or rather a mansion, of her own. The woman with expensive tastes had also bought two luxurious latest cars now. The most latest, a sports Benz, was simply classy.

The woman who had long personified beauty and charm now personified comfort and luxury as well. In actual fact, she loved to show off her riches. Anything fun and entertaining, sports especially, was her favourite pastime now. She again loved to attend social functions at which she always stole the show by her appearance and attractive cash and other presents.

The life of total fun and luxury was very therapeutic indeed. It was wonderfully soothing. It actually helped to suppress the humiliation that was associated with the woman's ordeal appreciably. Unfortunately, it was only a mirage. The fun and luxury therapy could not provide a lasting solution to her problems. As the saying goes, 'A rite that is performed with a drink cannot be performed with water to produce the same results'.

As time went by, the rich woman needed something that, in her opinion, all her riches could not compare. Auntie Serwaa felt the need for a child so strongly that she did not even care who the father must be. In fact, she did not care about his identity, looks or any other considerations. She just needed a child, and that was all.

Although the idea of adoption crossed her mind, she debunked it at once. To all intents and purposes, she felt that it could not be differentiated from childlessness. The woman again believed that even if it could, it would always remind her of the bitter truth. Besides, she strongly believed that she was not infertile and thus she deserved to have her own child.

Preoccupied with the dream that seemed far-fetched, Auntie Serwaa felt that the business could be left in a shambles. She thus found the employment of a manager worthwhile. The woman eventually employed a professional, a very dynamic and responsible man, to take the position. The man in early middle age was assisted by a young woman who was a former waitress. She also happened to be the first employee.

At present, the woman had learnt to be very generous, especially to her household. She had been assisting her needy co-tenants and others in various ways but mostly financially. There was one poor widow in the house to whom she was most generous. Daavi Kyekena, who was an Ewe woman, could never forget to be indebted to the kind woman. Her husband had died untimely prior to Auntie Serwaa's relocation. The late businessman had died a pauper after his cargoes of contraband goods had been impounded and destroyed.

The benefactor, after learning about the poor woman's widowhood, decided to be supportive. She quickly set her up in a petty trade and again offered to pay her children's school fees. The kind woman did many other things that really helped to alleviate the family's poverty.

One good turn, it is said, deserves another. Without any husband or children, Daavi had suspected that her benefactor must have a problem. She strongly felt that the woman must be infertile. But she believed that the priest of Kateka, the powerful god in her region, could be of help. The Volta Region, the home of the Ewe tribe, was noted for its spiritual powers that were vested in the traditional priests and priestesses by the gods. She, however, wondered how best she could approach her about her suspicions without putting their relationship in jeopardy. Auntie Serwaa had never opened up to her before. Besides, she seemed unfriendly and rather difficult to approach. But the poor woman could not afford to lose her gestures of support.

The concerned widow remained in a quandary for a while. Then one evening, while she kept wondering about the woman, she summoned up courage and approached her. Then, diplomatically, she succeeded in engaging her in a conversation.

> Daavi: "Something about you has bothered me for a while, Auntie Serwaa. But I don't seem to have the courage to talk to you about it. I actually wonder if it won't jeopardise our relationship."
>
> Auntie Serwaa: "I've really gone through hell in life, Daavi. What I've been through in life is

undreamt-of. You won't believe me if I shared any of my experiences with you. Presently, I don't think any other experience will be unendurable. So feel free and go ahead, Daavi."

Daavi: "Thank you, Auntie. Emm, emm, I've noticed that no one visits you - no husband, no children. Is there any problem, Auntie?"

Auntie Serwaa: "Hmm, thanks for your concern, Daavi. Yes, there's a problem, a very big one, actually. I can't have children."

Daavi: "Ooh, that's too bad, Auntie. Anyway, I don't think it's too late yet. There's a god in my area that's very powerful and can be of help. It has helped many women who were said to be barren, including a friend of mine, to have babies. I can take you there if you wouldn't mind."

Auntie Serwaa: "Of course, I wouldn't, Daavi. Just tell me when you can take me there and I'll be ready."

Daavi: "I'm ever ready, Auntie. I can even take you there tomorrow, and that's if it'll be convenient to you."

Auntie Serwaa: "Sure, so it's a deal."

Daavi: "OK, Auntie. But we'll have to set off at dawn, maybe around four, so we can make a return journey."

Auntie Serwaa: "Your wish's my command, Daavi. I'm very grateful indeed."

Daavi: "Don't mention it, Auntie."

The women left Oseikrom for Anglokor the following morning and arrived around noon. As they approached the abode of the celebrated ancient god, the woman whose hopes had been raised remained expectant. The one who had shown passionate concern for her bene-factor's ordeal led the way while the latter followed her closely. Finally, they got to the antique enclosure and entered very cautiously. They greeted everyone around and then joined the queue. Since it was not a busy day, it soon got to their turn and the native led the stranger in.

Traditional Priest: "You are welcome, my mothers."
Auntie Serwaa: "Thank you, Nana."
Daavi: "Thank you, Wise One."
Traditional Priest: "I called you my mothers because every woman is a man's mother. By the way, how may the great god help you?"
Daavi: "My friend cannot have babies, Wise One. So we are here to seek the help of the benevolent god."
Traditional Priest: "Thank you very much for your kindness and compassion. May the great god I serve reward you abundantly. Now, if you would not mind, I would like to talk to your friend in private."
Daavi: "OK, Wise One. I am waiting outside."
Traditional Priest: "Good. I am going to be frank with you, my mother. There is no way you can have babies, because no real or living man can ever make love to you."

Auntie Serwaa: "But why, Wise One? How can a spirit marry a human being, or rather how can a ghost marry a human being, if I may ask?"
Traditional Priest: "Well, it is a real pity, my mother. But I am afraid it is not my job to provide an answer to such a teaser. Mine is to help you fix your problems. Unfortunately, this particular one is beyond my intervention. I am afraid there is nothing that I or any other intermediary between the spirits and humankind can do about your peculiar problem. You just have to learn to live with it. A word, as they say, is enough for the wise."
Auntie Serwaa: "Thank you, Wise One. And if you'll excuse me, I'll like to leave."
Traditional Priest: "Go in peace, my mother, and may the great god be your guide."
Auntie Serwaa: "Thank you, Wise One."

Auntie Serwaa returned to Oseikrom a disappointed woman. But she was still grateful to Daavi for her genuine compassion. She was especially thankful that she led her to a candid source that painted the real picture of her ordeal. And although she remained confused about the unexplained cause of it, she resolved to let things lie. Gradually, she managed to deal with the helpless emotions somehow and seemed quite content to stay unmarried and childless forever.

CHAPTER 18

Serwaa-Akoto Moves into Her Own House

Auntie Serwaa never ceased to be generous and compassionate. But there was one unhealthy behaviour she had to deal with, and that was hatred for her family. Surprisingly, she was still at loggerheads with them, her parents especially. She still felt that they were treacherous.

One afternoon, the poor couple paid her an unexpected visit. Yaa-Yaa had secretly given them the directions. Daavi Kyekena, on her way out of the house, happened to meet them right at the entrance. After they had greeted her, the man respectfully asked for Auntie Serwaa. Guessing they must be her parents, she quickly let them in. Then she proudly led them upstairs, straight to their daughter's door.

"Agoo! Agoo!" she knocked hard with her mouth as usual, smiling in great delight. "Please come out, Auntie!" she added briefly. "Your parents are here!"

Upon hearing of her parents' presence, the woman who simply loathed seeing her family flew into a fury. Then she dashed out of the room and banged the door rather crazily.

Auntie Serwaa: "Just go back to wherever you came from! You have no daughter to visit!"

Papa Gyabaa: "Please calm down, my daughter. We're your parents forever and nothing can change that. You just can't disown us. A child who disowns his or her family loses his or her identity. You don't have to be stubborn, please."

Naana Dumaa: "Heaven knows we've neither wronged nor hurt you, Serwaa. We still love you dearly and we'll forever do. Just allow us into your home and we shall thrash out any misunderstandings amicably. We can't wash our dirty linen in public."

Daavi: "I seem to be all at sea, Auntie Serwaa. But whatever the problem is, I think you should allow them in. After all, your parents remain your parents and nothing changes that. And just as your mother said, you can't wash your dirty linen in public."

Auntie Serwaa: "No, Daavi, I still insist they go away! I don't want to have anything to do with them now or ever! I hate them!"

Papa Gyabaa and his wife burst into helpless tears as their only daughter turned them away. Daavi was shocked at the woman's uncharitable behaviour towards her own parents. She really wondered how serious the problem could be. But in any case, she found the extent of the woman's misbehaviour outrageous. But what more could she say or do when her hands were tied? Definitely, she could not afford to bite the hand that fed her. She only consoled the poor couple and saw them off.

When she returned, she went back to the woman and tried to calm her down. Of course, she was as cautious as someone in a pair of white trousers walking along a muddy path.

Daavi: "Take it easy, Auntie. But you must try your utmost to let bygones be bygones."
Auntie Serwaa: "You may have misconstrued my actions and equated them to insolence, Daavi. But those couple deserved more than they received."
Daavi: "Hmm, well, that was so unlike you, anyway. But in any case, you still need to exercise restraint."
Auntie Serwaa: "Thanks, Daavi, but we'll see."

Now, at long last, Auntie Serwaa completed her house and was relocating soon. She was in a dilemma over two thoughts. The thought of moving in alone so she could enjoy total privacy seemed to reign supreme. However, she felt it was quite practical to move in with Daavi and her family so they would keep her company. After a period of critical thinking, she found the latter thought more reasonable. Shortly, she called the woman and discussed her good intentions with her.

Auntie Serwaa: "I'm moving to my new house pretty shortly, Daavi. And I was wondering if you and the children will move in with me. But if you ask me, you'll milk the relocation for all it's worth. First and foremost, it'll guarantee my continuous support. Second, the free accommodation will relieve your financial burden. And, of course, there'll be many other benefits. So what do you think?"
Daavi: "Wow! Well, to begin with, Congratulations on the completion of your house, Auntie."
Auntie Serwaa: "Thank you, Daavi."
Daavi: "And thank you very much for the offer."
Auntie Serwaa: "That's all right, Daavi."
Daavi: "It's a very great offer indeed, Auntie, and it's very, very thoughtful of you. Certainly, I can't say no to such an offer. But I hope we're moving in with your family, your parents at least."
Auntie Serwaa: "Oh Daavi, the peacemaker! Well, anyway, I've caught your meaning. You just don't want to be implicated in the dispute. Hmm, maybe you've got a point. But let's move in first and afterwards the issue about my family can be considered."

Daavi: "No, Auntie, first things first. I suggest you reconcile with the family first, then my children and I can move in with you."

Auntie Serwaa: "Oh well, Daavi, I can see your stubborn streak. Well, maybe you don't need my assistance anymore. So you can continue to stay here, but I'm gone shortly."

On that note, the conversation ceased and the woman entered the bedroom without ceremony. She was very probably annoyed. But poor Daavi, quite confused, remained in the sofa and pretended to be watching the television. Shortly, she got a clearer meaning of what the woman said and got worried as well. On reflection, however, she felt that she had acted in good faith and calmed down. Then some seconds later, and rather abruptly, she left the room feeling no remorse for her response.

A few days later, Auntie Serwaa moved alone into her new house in Batabi. It was as magnificent as a castle. But the location, a developing residential area, was very quiet and virtually lonely. "I said I wouldn't need any company here," she said to herself one moment, "but certainly not that of a watchman."

Shortly, she obtained a placard from an artist's workshop. It read: 'A Full-Time Watchman Urgently Needed'. She tied it onto the gate and remained hopeful.

The next morning, one good-looking young man knocked on the gate and expressed interest in the job. But the informal interview that was done within a moment proved him unsuitable for it. The results were virtually abysmal. Again, judging him by intuition, the woman felt she could not employ him for reasons of mistrust.

About a week later or thereabouts, a middle-aged man came to the house and expressed keen interest in the job. He actually begged for it and was even ready to sacrifice his pay. "I'm not too interested in the pay, Madam," he said quite ridiculously. "Just house and feed me - that's all." In fact, the degree of the man's interest in, and readiness for, the menial job was to absurd lengths.

Auntie Serwaa: "You sound desperate, Papa. But I'll take that as proof of your readiness to live up to my expectations. However, you must give me some time to come to a decision. Please, come back the day after next for the final response."
Man: "Your wish is my command, Madam."
Auntie Serwaa: "By the way, what's your name?"
Man: "Yaro Baba - that's my full name. But you may call me Baba."
Auntie Serwaa: "OK. See you later then."
Man: "See you later, Madam."

The ageing man who seemed desperate for a job went back and returned in three days' time. Now, the woman had finalised her decision. Having made some discreet enquiries about him, she felt that she could safely employ him.

Auntie Serwaa: "I'm ready to give you the job, Papa. I'll pay you good salary and provide your basic needs, including a decent accommodation. But no wife or children will visit you here. I need total privacy. That's the only condition."

Man: "No problem, Madam. I neither have a wife nor a child. I'm a confirmed bachelor."

Auntie Serwaa: "A confirmed bachelor? Are you sure?"

Man: "Very sure, Madam."

Auntie Serwaa: "That's interesting anyway. By the way, you said your name was……?"

Man: "Yaro Baba, Madam. But you can call me Baba."

Auntie Serwaa: "OK. That's a nice name anyway. And I guess you're a Muslim?"

Man: "No, I'm not, Madam. I'm just a Gao man from northern Nigeria."

Auntie Serwaa: "Oh I see. But you don't look like a Gao man at all. I guessed your tribe as Akan at first sight. But that's no bother at all. You can move in tomorrow and start work."

Man: "Thank you, Madam, but I'm not going back. I'm ready to start work at once. All my belongings are here with me. Everything I've ever owned is in this small bag."

Auntie Serwaa: "Wow! Wonders will never cease. Anyway, you'll live in the boys' quarters. I'll soon get you the keys. And a motorbike will be at your disposal. But I hope you can ride it?"

Man: "Yes, Madam. I really ride well, even on horses. By the way, thank you very much once again. May Allah bless you."

Auntie Serwaa: "Don't mention it, Baba, and Amen to your prayer."

Auntie Serwaa called Baba the following morning and gave him a few instructions. "Don't ever let anyone in, not even an angel, without my permission," she said sternly. "Every visitor waits at the gate while you seek my consent to let them in. And if anyone trespasses, deal with him or her mercilessly. You have my unqualified backing on whatever actions you take against a trespasser."

"Your wish's my command, Madam," Baba said humbly. Then, looking a little funny in his gear, he returned to work and made sure he was impressive. In particular, he ensured that he followed all the instructions strictly.

Exactly three weeks after her relocation Daavi Kyekena decided to pay her a visit. Perhaps her purpose was to check on her benefactor at her new place. As usual, the watchman asked her to wait at the gate while he sought the mistress' consent.

Baba: "Excuse me, Madam. One Daavi is at the gate. Can she come in?"

Auntie Serwaa: "No, she can't. Tell her none of my family lives with me yet and so she can't come in."

The man went back and gave the message to the woman virtually verbatim. But Daavi was not too surprised at it. After all, she could still remember the full treatment she meted out to her own parents vividly. But, genuinely, she pitied her 'living alone' in such a very big house. She felt that she was losing the novelty of companionship because of her unforgiving character. However, she learnt her lesson and never made any attempt to visit her again.

Some months later, the woman's family, her parents and brothers, came knocking at her gate. Since she was not at home at present, the watchman decided to exercise his discretion in allowing or denying them entry. He humbly found out about who they were as well as their purpose there.

"We're Serwaa-Akoto's family," Papa Gyabaa replied. "We're here to visit her." Then, smiling faintly, he went ahead and made the introductions briefly. "I'm her father, this is her mother, and the young men are her brothers," he said.

"All right then, you're welcome home," the watchman said warmly. "Please, come in and make yourselves comfortable. Madam will be back very soon."

The man proudly led the family in and offered them a place to sit. For a moment, they were all owls. Every single one of them was palpably consumed by curiosity. With their eyes widely open and unblinking, they turned their necks around many times in a twinkling. Everyone was clearly taken aback by the woman's impressive achievement.

Soon, the mistress signalled her arrival. As usual, she sounded her horn two times consecutively. Then Baba, unable to hide his smiles, rushed to open the gate. But before he could say anything, the woman spotted the family seated under the summer hut and all hell broke loose.

Auntie Serwaa: "Didn't I ask you to deal mercilessly with any trespasser, Baba?"
Baba: "Yes, you did, Madam."
Auntie Serwaa: "Then what're those people doing there? You'd better chase them out now!"
Baba: "But they said they were your family, Madam."
Auntie Serwaa: "They said they were whose family? I don't know any one of them from Adam! Just do as I said, Baba! Chase them out now!"
Baba: "Yes, Madam."

Speechless, to say the least, the family had no option but to follow each other out, just like ants. As they headed towards the gate, the watchman, obeying the order to the letter, straggled behind the last person in stunned silence. Then, rather crazily, the woman quickly picked a broom and swept away their footprints while they headed out. Afterwards, she had a bone to pick with the watchman.

"You're fired for not living up to my expectations, Baba!" she yelled angrily. "Now go and pack all your belongings and leave my house at once!"

But the man was total humility before the angry woman. He quickly lay before her, virtually prostrating, and held her feet with both hands. Then he took the blame with deep regret and made an apology.

Having beaten his breast, the woman was finally moved to forgive him. She hesitantly held him by the hands and helped him up. But something sickening, or perhaps ridiculous, followed shortly. Auntie Serwaa and the watchman suddenly fell in love, kissed and made love sequentially.

Immediately upon the lovemaking, the woman suddenly remembered something. "There is no way you can have babies, because no real or living man can ever make love to you."

At once, she felt that Yaro Baba could not be a real human being. She thought that he must be a ghost or some other spirit in human form. "But why did I stoop to allow my watchman to make love to me in the first place?" she wondered. "No, that wasn't me. Or did he cast a spell on me?"

Ironically, it never occurred to her to chase the spirit of a watchman out of the house. She was never scared of him either. The only problem she seemed to have about the bizarre affair which did not even stop was negative self-image. Of course, she found the man an apology for a husband or even a mere partner. However, she felt helpless to do anything about the apparent relationship. So they continued to cohabit while the woman continued to wrestle with a sense of shame and unease.

The Misunderstanding Between Her Parents

It had been more than a month since the family were thrown out of Auntie Serwaa's house. But her poor father was still depressed about the bitter experience. He could not bear to think about it, especially the fact that it was a second-time experience. Now, he could hardly eat anything and had had to work up an appetite, or his wife would have a bone to pick with him. Certainly, no wife would tolerate her husband's virtual refusal of her meals, supper especially, without any reasonable excuse. He became increasingly gloomy when it kept occurring to him every so often that they were likely to be rejected by the woman forever. Naana Dumaa was bothered by her cheerful husband's cheerless mood.

Naana Dumaa: "You've not been yourself for a while, Papa Gyabaa. You look troubled and dejected. Is anything the matter, my gentlemanly husband?"

Papa Gyabaa: "But how can I feel myself when all isn't well with the only daughter we have? And more especially when she doesn't even want to have anything to do with us, the only family she has."

Naana Dumaa: "But you can't worry so much about that girl's misbehaviour, my darling. After all, she chose to disown us, not the other way round. And Heaven knows we've tried our best in vain to have her reconciled with us. As far as I'm concerned, she even owes us apologies, and the earlier she realises that the better."

Papa Gyabaa: "Well, it appears you still haven't caught the real meaning of your daughter's actions, Maame Dumaa. You see, my dear, in the context of her circumstance, the strange behaviour or 'misbehaviour', as you usually put it, was quite justifiable. There's no smoke without fire, as they say. She just can't accept to pay the price for something she knows nothing about, someone else's costly mistake."

Naana Dumaa: "What're you trying to insinuate, Papa Gyabaa? Are you now blaming me for your daughter's problems?"

Papa Gyabaa: "I'm not just insinuating, Maame Dumaa, I'm telling the real truth."

Naana Dumaa: "And what is the real truth, Papa Gyabaa?"

Papa Gyabaa: "You'd better stop the pretence, Maame Dumaa, for the truth is as clear as day. Who doesn't know that our daughter's problems are linked to your refusal to marry the Gao man?"

Naana Dumaa: "Don't you dare make me lose my temper, Papa Gyabaa! You know me well and so you daren't push me! After all, you knew about all that and perhaps many others before you made the choice to marry me. I can still remember vividly that your parents even warned you against the decision. So why did you go ahead and married me when you knew it was bound to be problematic? Please, my darling, don't go any further, or you'll be asking for trouble."

Papa Gyabaa: "But what makes you think I'm scared by your rage, Maame Dumaa? Anyhow, yes, my late parents did warn me sternly. But you see, my dear, I was so charmed and blinded by your looks that I turned a deaf ear to all that they said. But they've been proven right after all. "

Naana Dumaa: "You are very ingenuous and inglorious indeed, Papa Gyabaa. I never knew you were such a naughty gentleman. And I swear by my late parents' graves, I'll summon you before the Council of Elders. Perhaps you'll explain yourself more clearly there."

Papa Gyabaa: "I know what I'm talking about and I can't be scared by your empty threats. You can go ahead and summon me anywhere. You can even summon me before Otumfuor, the great King of the Asante Kingdom, for all I care."

Despite the suspicions her appalling fate had aroused, especially in her home town, Auntie Serwaa knew nothing about the secret about her family yet. The very big secret was unknown to her quadruplet brothers either. It appeared that everyone, including even the blabbermouths, had found it difficult to let them in on the top family secret. But perhaps it was bound to be discovered one day. After all, the moon cannot hide behind the clouds forever.

Presently, the quadruplets were all eligible bachelors. They were all good-looking gentlemen who were well mannered. Additionally, they were all hard-working and independent economically. Marriage, one of the chief measures of how man enough a man was in the rural community, was clearly long overdue for each of them. Sadly, none of them was even in any serious relationship yet. But just like their sister's that was even more serious, the people were not the least bit baffled by the bizarre situation. After all, they had their suspicions.

A day after the little misunderstanding between the couple, in the morning, the man received a summons from the palace. He was about to leave for the shop when a herald brought the urgent message. It said that the Chief and the Council of Elders were meeting with him in the evening. It quickly added that he ought to be there in time and without fail.

All the while Papa Gyabaa was furious inwardly. The message was actually received with suppressed resentment. The fact was, he flew into a fury the moment the young man appeared. He could guess that the woman had actually lodged the complaint she had threatened him with. He only managed to pretend composure as a mark of respect for the Stool and the august Council.

Obviously, there was a mood swing immediately upon the herald was gone. Itching to scold the troublemaker of a wife, the enraged husband could hardly control himself.

Papa Gyabaa: "You are a very big disappointment indeed, Maame Dumaa! But how could you do such a disgraceful thing, for Christ's sake? Then I guess I must do the worst so you would have enough hard evidence against me! I guess I must disfigure your ugly face at once!"
Naana Dumaa: "Why don't you kill me and have peace of mind, Papa Gyabaa! At least be man enough for once and go ahead and strangle me! Useless man!"
Tawia: "Oh no, Maame, that was below the belt. It was uncalled for. The two of you'd better stop the argument now, for goodness' sake!"

Papa Gyabaa: "Oh, allow her to throw insults at me! Just allow the quarrelsome old witch to hurl insults at me and I'll turn her into a punchbag."
Tawia: "Oh, Papa! I never knew you were so temperamental. But a man should learn to control his temper, or he'll always be landed in trouble. Whatever the problem is, I entreat you to let restraint be your watchword. You both must calm down, please."
Papa Gyabaa: "You certainly don't know the woman you call your mother too well, Tawia. You'd understand me better if you did. That mother of yours is quarrelsome, unforgiving and, most of all, domineering. That's the dark side to your mother's character, my son. She's really treacherous and I regret ever getting married to such a woman."
Naana Dumaa: "Then divorce me at once! Just go ahead and divorce me now, Papa Gyabaa! I'm sick and tired of your querulous character!"

Now, the worsening of the situation was quite foreseeable. The heightening tension was clear evidence. To forestall any such scenario, the young man who happened to be the only person at the scene had to act smartly. He tried his best and succeeded in persuading his father and taking him out. He eventually succeeded in calming him down and then escorting him to the workplace.

Papa Gyabaa closed from work quite early and as usual went home first of all. And although supper had already been served, he refused to eat. Obviously, he was still angry with the cook who was even not around. He only freshened up and then headed straight for the palace.

The revered Council that was chaired by the Chief had just seated when he arrived. Not surprisingly, his wife was there. She had been seated facing the traditional court. As usual, he bowed and greeted the Chief first and then the others. Afterwards, he was asked to sit by his wife. A chair was already waiting. Shortly, the Chief asked Nana 'Kyeame, the linguist, to commence the meeting.

> Linguist: "You are welcome, Papa Gyabaa, and may we know your purpose here."
> Papa Gyabaa: "Thank you, Nana 'Kyeame. I crave your permission to speak, 'Nananom'. I had a message in the morning that Nana and his Elders needed me around this time. In short, I am here in response to the summons."
> Linguist: "You heard him state his purpose briefly, Nana and Elders."
> Chief: "Right. You may tell him why he was summoned, Nana 'Kyeame."
> Linguist: "Your wife was here the other day, and she lodged a complaint that you abused her verbally. She said that you even threatened her with physical abuse as well. What do you have to say, Papa Gyabaa?"

Papa Gyabaa: "I am sorry, Nana and Elders, but I am highly disappointed in my wife for behaving rather childishly. First and foremost, she did not need to wash our dirty linen in public. The problem we had was a normal misunderstanding between a husband and a wife. It was even trivial and did not deserve your attention whatsoever. In fact, 'Nananom', there was no need bothering this august Council with such a trivial matter. I do not intend to wash our dirty linen in public too, 'Nananom'. But I think I should be allowed to let the cat out of the bag in order to explain myself more clearly."

Linguist: "You may go ahead, Papa Gyabaa. After all, we need the facts to enable us make good judgements."

Papa Gyabaa: "Thank you, Nana 'Kyeame. I hope you can still recollect the curse that was put on my wife's family many years ago, 'Nananom'?"

Elders: "Oh yes, we can! In fact, we do vividly recall everything."

Papa Gyabaa: "Thank you, 'Nananom'. I hope you would again recollect how mysteriously her late parents met their doom?"

Linguist: "Of course, everyone does, Papa Gyabaa. You had better stop beating about the bush."

Papa Gyabaa: "I am sorry, Nana 'Kyeame, but I was only trying to arrive at a point. Anyhow, my late parents did warn me against marrying her but

I would not listen. I was blinded by love. But now, the effects of the curse have finally dawned on me. Our only daughter who clearly personifies beauty and grace can neither marry nor have babies."
Some Elders: "Mmm? This is very pitiful indeed. But why, Papa Gyabaa?"
Papa Gyabaa: "Hmm, 'Nananom', no man has ever succeeded in marrying her. As a matter of fact, 'Nananom', and with all apologies, no man has even ever succeeded in sleeping with her, except spirits."
Elders: "What! But that is impossible, Papa Gyabaa!"
Papa Gyabaa: "Hmm, 'Nananom', that is exactly the case. And every attempt at seeking a solution has only been futile. Now, our only daughter has disowned us; she has disowned the entire family, even. She has also banished herself from the village because of the ordeal. I cannot even remember when she last set foot in this village. And look at my sons too, 'Nananom'. They are all very handsome, very hard-working and financially sound. But no woman in this village wants to accept to marry them. And, apparently, it has got to do with the same curse. As a man, the head of my family, how do people expect me to feel? Is it not only natural that I would some-times react to the issue the way I did, 'Nananom'? Well, anyway, I am done. Thank you."
Some Elders: "It is very pitiful indeed, Papa Gyabaa. But just take it easy. Everything will be fine."

Linguist: "You heard it all, Nana and Elders."
Chief: "Ask the complainant if she has got anything to say regarding her husband's lengthy explanation."
Linguist: "I hope you heard your husband right, Naana Dumaa. What is your reaction to what he said?"
Naana Dumaa: "I ask your permission to speak, Nana and Elders. In fact, all that my husband said was right, except the linkage he made between our children's circumstance and the supposed curse on the family. You would all bear me out, 'Nananom', that destiny is equally capable of bringing misfortune."
Some Elders: "Oh yes, surely!"
Naana Dumaa: "I rest my case, 'Nananom'. Thank you."
Linguist: "You heard her brief response, 'Nananom'."
Chief: "Ask them to excuse the Council for a moment, Okyeame. They can make themselves comfortable in the waiting room."
Linguist: "Kindly excuse us for a moment. Please, follow me to the waiting room."

The Council of Elders' Ultimatum

The linguist led the family to the waiting room and asked them to make themselves comfortable. Then he went back to the hall to partake in the deliberations.

Chief: "I can sense danger, Elders. The whole community could be awaiting destruction. No doubt the family's misfortune is a peculiar manifestation of the effects of the lineal curse. And now that virtually all of them have had their fair share, we can't afford to be unconcerned, 'Nananom'. Instinct tells me that curse could spell doom for the whole community if we do not make the right move now."
Elder I: "You have spoken very well indeed, Nana. In fact, we do not need any seer to tell us there is doom ahead. We have to act fast and now. That is my brief suggestion."

Elder II: "I will not mince words in branding that accursed family as hoodoo, Nana. And they need to be ostracised, in my opinion."
Elder III: "There is only one best action to take, Nana; and all that the others have said alludes to that. They must be banished - that is all!"
Most of the Elders: "Exactly, Nana! He has hit the nail right on the head!"
Chief: "I have heard the majority view, Elders. But we need to be cautious about the approach in order to avoid mistakes and blame for that matter. We should not lose sight of the fact that the evidence we have gathered so far is only suggestive and not proven. But I think I know what to do. You may call them back, Nana 'Kyeame."

The linguist went back to the waiting room and returned shortly with the couple.

Linguist: "Welcome back, Papa and Maame Gyabaa."
Couple: "Thank you, Nana 'Kyeame."
Chief: "Tell them on behalf of the Council, Okyeame, that we find the strange happenings in the family significant. They are a loud wake-up call to them, us and the entire village for that matter to act promptly to reverse the curse that was put on them a while long ago. Tell them a stitch in

time saves nine. So the Council has resolved to give them a maximum of twelve calendar months within which the curse must be reversed. Tell them again that the only evidence we shall accept for the total reversal of the curse is the marriage of their children, their daughter especially. That is the decision of the Council."

Linguist and Elders: "Well done, Nana. Everything was in order."

Linguist: "You heard the Council's decision loud and clear, Papa and Maame Gyabaa. Do you have anything to say in response?"

Papa Gyabaa: "Please, Okyeame, tell Nana and the rest of the Council that we shall do our utmost to meet the deadline. We cannot afford to incur the displeasure of the Council. May the gods and the ancestors of our land have mercy on us. Thank you."

Linguist: "'Nananom' have heard you very clearly, and we wish you well. At this juncture, you have our leave to leave."

Couple: "Thank you, Nana 'Kyeame."

The family's house was hell on earth that fateful evening. The man broke the news to his sons as soon as they got home and they all felt very disappointed in their mother. They felt that she had gone overboard with her complaints. They were particularly disturbed by the Council's ultimatum which they found rather demeaning. The quadruplets again felt that it was potentially problematic.

"Now, you've fed us to the lions, Maame," Tawia said.

"Yes!" Papa Gyabaa added. "And there'll be hell to pay!"

Regretful, obviously, the woman could not utter a word in defence of the drastic action. She only looked disconcerted and ashamed before her sons who loathed being pressured. But there was no way she could turn the clock back and make amends.

Having remained dumb for a while, Naana Dumaa finally spoke. Now, the tension in the house had subsided somewhat. Sadly, and rather childishly, she only rubbed salt in a wound.

"But you can't blame me for everything," she said, pulling a face and trying to win her sons' sympathy. "Your father too deserves a portion of it. After all, it was his actions that compelled me to lodge the complaint. But your late grandparents, my parents, deserve the lion's share. They were the ones who struck the deal that led to my birth and eventually the cursing of the family. They were just short-sighted and selfish. Or perhaps……"

"You have no shame one little bit, Maame Dumaa!" Papa Gyabaa interrupted in annoyance. "Oh keep on - keep on sharing the blame you're supposed to take alone! After all, your late parents cannot speak in their defence! And I'm not ready to face the Council again, at least not now! But if I were you, I'd remain bowed in shame forever! Shameless woman!"

"Oh, Papa," Nyank, the last of the quadruplets, said softly, "and Maame too - this is certainly not the time to quarrel. It isn't the time to blame either. We'd better consider how best we can get the supposed panacea to our problems and perhaps the whole village's done."

"So, what do you suggest, Nyank?" Ata Panin asked rather curiously. He was the oldest among the quadruplets.

"I think……" Nyank attempted to say something.

"The one who ties the knot must know best how to untie it," Papa Gyabaa, still bitter about his wife's behaviour, cut in. "Let that troublesome mother of yours make the first suggestion."

"You must calm down, Papa, please!" Ata Kakra yelled rather harshly. "It's only human to err after all!" He was getting bored with his father's endless reproach.

The family finally decided to trace the herbalist to his roots. Unfortunately, the woman could not remember anything about him, except his name. Everything else remained elusive. But, obviously, his name alone could not be a dependable lead. Having already made an intuitive guess that he must be dead by now, they needed enough details to facilitate the arduous task. The woman really needed to keep racking her brains.

Although the strong likelihood of the man's death stared them in the face, they were neither discouraged nor worried. They were actually prepared for any eventuality and that was without exception. They believed that even finding a relative of his could make a great deal of difference to their situation.

After quite a while, Naana Dumaa remembered something else that could be of help. Now, there was the need for a consensus. They all had to agree that the expedition could be undertaken with the scanty details without much difficulty. And when they eventually did, they quickly decided on a date.

Preparations for the journey to the unknown destination got underway at once. The family prudently planned for a fortnight's journey at least. Thus, it took them a few days to get set.

The next Monday, at the crack of dawn, the family set out on a long journey to Buipe. According to Naana Dumaa, that was the place her late mother had once said she met the man.

While they were on their way, she deliberately fell into conversation with an old woman she sat by on the bus. The funny old lady, a northerner who mentioned her name as Koloma, was very forthcoming. Sadly, she could not express herself well in Twi, the southerner's mother tongue which was incidentally the most widely used language. She explained she had had only a passing acquaintance with the Asante people. But she was still able to have a meaningful conversation with the woman who was desperate for a solution to her family's problems.

She gave her useful clues to finding the man or any relatives of his in case he was no more.

The family stuck to the few clues in all their enquiries when they eventually arrived at their destination. They were thus directed to four different villages, all of which turned out to be wrong places. Before they were aware, they had trekked several kilometres along some dangerous, virtually impassable routes fruitlessly. Now, they were all tired and their impatience was growing. However, they were not despaired. The quadruplets especially were optimistic about their eventual success.

The poor family ended up resting under a shed at the main station. Now, there seemed to be some confusion as to what to do again. But the woman knew that everything rested with her to conjure up additional useful details. She suddenly found herself in a dream and before long the name of a particular village struck her. She was quite sure her late mother had once mentioned it in passing in relation to her fateful birth. She was, however, not sure about the accuracy of the pronunciation.

"I've just remembered something - the name of a village," she said. "I'm quite sure my late mother once said she would take me to Kankan to visit a man, a herbalist. She never did, though. And I think he must be the one we're looking for. But I wonder if I got the pronunciation correctly."

"Then let's get someone to confirm it," Papa Gyabaa suggested. "After all, there's no harm in trying."

Quickly, he left them and approached a man, a driver or a driver's mate perhaps, who was leaning against a stationary bus.

Papa Gyabaa: "Excuse me, Sir. Please, do you by any chance know of a village by the name of Kankan?"
Man: "I'm sorry, Papa, but I haven't heard that name before. You may ask someone else about it."
Papa Gyabaa: "OK, Sir. Thanks for your kindness anyway."
Man: "That's all right."

Shortly, Papa Gyabaa found another man. He seemed to be a 'mallam', an Arabic teacher, judging by how he was dressed. And he suddenly had a premonition that he could give some real lead.

Papa Gyabaa: "Good evening, Sir. Oh sorry, good evening, 'Mallam'."
Man 2: "'Awo', 'awo'."
Papa Gyabaa: "Do you please know of any village by the name of Kankan?"
Man 2: "Uui, 'Sante Papa, you said Kankan instead of Kanana. There's no village called Kankan here, but there's one called Kanana."
Papa Gyabaa: "Mmm? OK. But where can I find it, please?"

Man 2: "Uui, Papa! It's quite late and the road is rough and quite dangerous. You can spend the night here and continue your journey tomorrow."
Papa Gyabaa: "OK, 'Mallam'. Thanks. But how can I get there? Where's the station?"
Man 2: "Just there. (He pointed to it.) You'll pick a car there tomorrow morning."
Papa Gyabaa: "OK. Thank you very much, 'Mallam'."
Man 2: "Uui, Papa! I'm not a 'mallam'; I've never taught Arabic before. I'm only a tailor. And my name is Iddi, Iddi Sori."
Papa Gyabaa: "Oh sorry - sorry for calling you by that misnomer."
Man 2: "That's all right, Papa."
Papa Gyabaa: "Anyhow, I'm Papa Gyabaa. I'm from the south. I'm pleased to meet you."
Man 2: "I'm pleased to meet you too."

The man went back looking rather worried. He sighed pitifully and then said hopelessly: "No one said they knew any village by such a name in this whole land. But the last man I talked to mentioned something closer. What did he even say? Ahaa, Kanana - that was what he said."

"He must be right!" the woman yelled cheerfully. "Yes! Yes! That was it! Kanana was the village my mother said we would visit!"

"Then the problem is half solved," her husband said pleasantly. "We only need to clear the hurdle of locating the place, that's all."

"But that's happening tomorrow by hook or by crook, Papa," Tawia remarked confidently.

"Sure!" his brothers added, quite confidently too.

Sadly, the family had to spend the night under the shed, the bamboo structure that was roofed with palm fronds. Each of them used one of the benches that had been mounted for passengers to improvise a bed on which they lay. None of them had a bit of sound sleep, for everyone spent most of the night daydreaming. Besides, the night police, those noisy vampires of insects, made much of a nuisance of themselves.

CHAPTER 21

The Dilemma of the Family

The following morning, as early as possible, the family set out again and hopefully. They boarded the only minibus they found at the station and crossed their fingers. The car which had no roadworthy sticker was as rickety as an egg. Interestingly, it was the only bus that plied the rough road that linked the town and the cluster of villages of which their destination was one.

About half an hour later or so, they eventually arrived at Kanana and none of the passengers could be recognised. Every one of them was completely shrouded in dust.

"What a journey to remember forever!" Panin exclaimed jokingly, and all the family giggled to break the boredom.

"Let's enter an old house in ruins and ask after the man," Kakra suggested, seemingly jokingly too. But, interestingly, they all lauded it. So, as though they knew their way around, they walked confidently through the narrow, serpentine streets looking for any house that fitted in with their preference. They neither greeted nor talked to anyone, prompting a good deal of speculation.

They finally entered one dilapidated house that seemed to have had some glory in the past and met two young men and an old one.

Family: "Good morning, gentlemen."

Men: "'Awo'."

Papa Gyabaa: "Please, we're looking for the some-time famous herbalist by the name of Baba Sakawa, or any of his relations."

Young men: "Uui! There's nobody by that name in this whole village, Papa."

Old man: "What are they looking for?"

Young man 1: "They're looking for one Baba Sakawa, a one-time veteran herbalist, or any relatives of his."

Old man: "Uui, 'Sante Papa! That will be very, very difficult, if not impossible. That man is long dead."

Papa Gyabaa: "Well, we made that presumption before the start of our journey, old man. But do you by any chance know any relatives of his who are still alive?"

Old man: "Uui! They all left the village after their breadwinner passed away. But I later learnt that one of his sons, his successor, had become a powerful traditional priest in Wangaro. You may go there and ask after him if you wish."

Papa Gyabaa: "Sure, we're there tomorrow, old man. By the way, thank you very much. We're very grateful indeed. Now, if you'll excuse us, we have to get going."

Old man: "You may leave in peace, 'Sante Papa and his family. I wish you the best of luck."

Family: "Thank you, old one."

The young men gave them concise directions to Wangaro while they were seeing them off. Quite excited now, the family were there the following morning. Tindaana, the owner of the land, was the only god in the whole community, so they were directed to his abode straightaway. A wave of expectancy engulfed them as they approached the sacred cottage, each of them crossing their fingers for good luck.

As soon as they entered the rather scary, antiquated cottage, they saw an old-looking priest whose mere appearance rekindled their hope. "He surely must be the one, judging by his age and……" they kept discussing in whispers as they got closer.

Traditional Priest: "Who did you say I must be, lovely family?"

Papa Gyabaa: "Good morning, 'mallam', emm, Baba."

Traditional Priest: "Good morning, 'Sante Papa. You may call me Neene."
Papa Gyabaa: "Thank you, Neene. Please, are you the son of Baba Sakawa, the one-time famous herbalist who once lived in Kanana?"
Traditional Priest: "You are at the right place, 'Sante Papa. Please, make yourselves comfortable on the benches and then we can get down to business."
Family: "Thank you, Neene."

The visitors quickly sat facing the man and remained attentive. Their momentary apprehension was clearly discernible on their expressive faces.

Traditional Priest: "The curse my late father put on your wife's family is reversible. But the price is as huge as the problem itself. Forewarned, as they say, is forearmed."
Papa Gyabaa: "Thank you very much, Neene. At least there is light on the horizon. But may we know what the price is?"
Traditional Priest: "No problem, I am coming to it. My late father's covenant with your late mother-in-law gave her a baby girl, your wife to be specific. But there was a breach of covenant afterwards, and that resulted in the curse that was put on the family. In short, there is only one option for its reversal, and

that is human sacrifice. You will need the head as well as the heart of a virgin for the rites."

Family: "Ei, Neene!"

Papa Gyabaa: "But you cannot rub salt in a wound, Neene. There is no way we can pay such a price. You just have to do your utmost to be helpful, please. There must be an alternative by hook or by crook, Neene."

Traditional Priest: "I am sorry, 'Sante Papa, but that is the only condition. After all, your own adage says: 'A rite that is performed with a drink cannot be performed with water to produce the same results'. Considerate as usual, I would have helped you out with any better alternative."

Papa Gyabaa: "OK. Thank you, Neene. And if you will excuse us, we shall leave and perhaps return later."

Traditional Priest: "Sure, 'Sante Papa. Now, it rests with you to pay the price and everything will be fine."

Papa Gyabaa: "Thank you once again, Neene. We may come back."

Traditional Priest: "Just a minute, 'Sante Papa! I know you love your family very much, your only daughter especially. I know you love her so dearly that you would do anything to have her reconciled with the family. To be very candid with you, 'Sante Papa, you as an individual do not have any problem, for you are not under any curse. But being the head

of the family, it is only right and proper that you spearhead the undertaking. You must therefore be man enough to fulfil the condition on their behalf. And just to serve as a reminder, the Chief and the Council of Elders are still expectant. You may now leave in peace."
Papa Gyabaa: "Thank you, Neene."

None of the family could think straight after the brief encounter with the man. They should have felt relieved at least, having succeeded in locating the supposed solution to their ordeal at last. But the costly price that was supposed to be the only condition for their freedom from the curse got them terrified. They remained traumatised for a great while and later found themselves at a crossroads. While they found the need for their freedom pressing, they felt that the consequences of the payment of the price could be dire.

A few days later, Papa Gyabaa began to display indifference or perhaps cowardice. He suddenly felt that he could no longer risk putting his life in danger. "After all, I'm now acutely aware that I'm not under any curse," he felt. "So why should I meddle and plunge myself into trouble?" The man literally felt that it would be childish or perhaps stupid on his part to sign his own death warrant. So he finalised that he would back out.

He quickly got the extended family informed about it and sought their opinion. Not surprisingly, the whole family backed him on 'the rational decision', as they described it. Unknown to him, they had already contemplated advising him on the need for such a bold decision. They were only waiting for the opportune moment.

"The entire family has long reached a decision on offering a suggestion of this nature," the head of the family said. "But since issues of this sort are quite delicate, we decided to wait for a moment like this. So if you've finally come to your senses, you have our unflagging support. You've really made the best decision."

The following morning, when all the young men had left for work, the man poured out his decision to his wife.

"I can no longer put up with the shame that hangs over this family, Maame Dumaa," he began rather straight-forwardly. "Everyone in this village knows it's accursed, and I wouldn't want to have anything to do with it again. My mind's made up and I'm moving out today. I feel very uncomfortable living under the same roof with you and your children."

"But you can't abandon your family, Papa Gyabaa," the woman said tearfully, "especially now that there's light at the end of the tunnel."

"Well, Maame Dumaa," he replied quite harshly, "the light you claim to see at the end of the tunnel is too faint to give any hope. But how's the payment of that huge price possible? Or are you going to put your sons up to it? Well, in any case, let me keep my mouth shut.

After all, I'm moving out shortly and I'll play no part in any such move."

"Please don't desert us, my darling husband," she said pathetically. "You're all my children and I have got." All the while she was on bended knee pleading, her miserable look opening the floodgates to a mood swing on the man's part.

"Sorry, my dear," he said quite tearfully. "I'm very sorry indeed. But I can't change my mind."

Naana Dumaa never dreamt that the husband of her youth could ever threaten to abandon her, especially at that dark moment. But she believed he would surely come round. Meanwhile, she decided to treat him to his favourite supper. She actually felt the need to do something special to set the stage for a heart-to-heart. She quickly got all the necessaries ready and waited on the appropriate time.

Supper was eventually cooked and the table was set for one as usual. Then Naana Dumaa crossed her fingers for the treat to work wonders. Unluckily, the woman who seemed to have a magic touch failed totally on this occasion. The special move was not potent enough to yield results. She waited expectantly for days, but the man never returned home. Now, it was getting dusky and the food was getting cold. When she finally realised it was likely to go to waste, Panin was sent to call him.

Ata Panin hurried to the big tree under which the men played draughts. He was sure to find his father there since the game was his favourite as well as his close friends'. Sadly, he was disappointed. According to the men, the master of the game had not set foot there all day.

The firstborn quickly checked all the other favourite hangouts of his father in vain. Then something, instinct, told him to look for him in his family house. And although he followed his instincts promptly, he was not the least sure of finding him there. He knew for certain that the man would hardly spend ten minutes in that house.

But it turned out as a big surprise when he finally entered the house. Papa Gyabaa was there and was actually relaxing in an armchair. He had just finished eating and was picking his teeth. The man on an errand was totally confounded by the second discovery especially.

"Your wife needs you home now, Papa."
"What for, if I may ask?"
"Well, I wouldn't know, Papa. I guess you must go and find out yourself."
"Well, for your information, young man, I'm not going back to that house again. I've relocated to this place."
"You can't be serious, Papa!"
"Well, I'm very serious, Panin. Going back to that house will be the last thing I'll ever do."

"But you can't do this to us, Papa! This is the time we need you most, for goodness' sake! You can't desert us now, Papa. That won't be fair."

"Well, this is no abandonment, young man. You and your brothers are always welcome here. This place is your second home, actually."

"But what will become of our mother, Papa?"

"Leave that to us, young man. That's purely a marital issue."

"And what about your belongings, if I may ask?"

"Oh, you can keep them. I can't take a pin out of that house."

"But why, Papa? Why have you suddenly turned indifferent? Or are you acting out of cowardice?"

"Mind you don't go overboard, young man. You're talking to no other person than your father."

"Well, I'm sorry, Papa, but that seems to be the bitter truth."

The young man returned quickly and broke the news to his mother and brothers. Blissfully unaware of what had happened earlier, the young men remained speechless for a while. But their poor mother who was already distressed remained distraught, staring into space in apparent disbelief.

"Don't mind that man," Tawia remarked suddenly. "He's only displaying cowardice."

"That was exactly what I told him," Panin added.

Together, the quadruplets calmed their downhearted mother down and assured her of their unflagging love and support.

"He's left you because he isn't your blood," Nyank, who was so fond of his mother, said. "But we're your blood, and as the saying goes, 'Blood is thicker than water'. We can never desert you, Mother."

The others too said similar things in turn to pacify the desolate woman, the promise of their enduring love running through the poetry.

When night finally fell, the loving sons who had felt compelled to act cleverly to save face had a secret meeting.

Nyank: "We'd better make every effort to erase the family's reputation for misfortune all because of the curse on us."

Tawia: "You never said a truer word, Nyank. So what do we do, bros?"

Panin: "There certainly can't be any better move than making every effort to satisfy the supposed condition for the reversal of the curse. I suggest we look for a virgin for the sacrifice of salvation."

Kakra: "Hear! Hear! Surely, bros, we have no other option but to deal with the problem once and for all. As the saying goes, 'He who fights and runs away lives to fight another day'."

The others: "Hear! Hear!"

Panin: "Do I take that for a unanimous decision, bros?"
The others: "Of course yes!"
Panin: "Unique Brothers!"
The others: "Together we act, divided we don't!"

CHAPTER 22

Meeting the Condition for Their Freedom

A few weeks later, Naana Dumaa was invited by the Elders of her late father's family for a brief discussion. Unknown to her, there was a very sensitive issue in hand, the final decision of which was in her hands. Her husband had finally sent some reasonable amount of money to them for her compensation and divorce. That was in accordance with tradition, anyway.

Head of family: "Your husband has decided to compensate you with GH¢5,000.00 and divorce you subsequently. What do you suggest we do?"

Naana Dumaa: "Hmm, Uncle, this is really a bitter pill to swallow. This sudden decision of my husband is like a dream to me. But what can I do? After all, there is nothing a woman can do to please a man who no longer loves her. So let him do as he pleases. As

for the money, he can keep it. I don't think even a fortune can compensate for the loss of my marriage."
Elders: "Our sentiments exactly, our niece."
Head of family: "Hmm, Naana, I don't think any reasonable family will support the divorce of their niece without any good cause. But judging from the way that man sounded, nothing short of a miracle can save this marriage. So all that I can say on behalf of the family is take heart, and take consolation in your sons. Now, each one of them is your son as well as your husband. By the way, we shall return the money at once."
Naana Dumaa: "Thank you, Uncle, and thank you, the rest of my uncles. And if you'd excuse me, I must be on my way."
Head of family: "You may leave in peace, our niece. Give my regards to your four husbands."
Naana Dumaa: "Ha-ha-ha! I will, Uncle. Thank you."

Abanaba was a hard-working house help and the prime target for the human sacrifice. The confirmed virgin had lived with, and worked for, the Odonkor family for years. Now, she was virtually regarded as one of them. She usually fetched water alone from the far away Ananse Dokono stream every evening. Having learnt about the routine, the quadruplets decided to ambush and kidnap her and use her for their own ends. They secretly spied out a safe place along the fairly lonely footpath for the intended crime and remained hopeful.

Three days later, as part of the plan, the men spied on the poor young woman all day. They became more anxious and alert after midday and had to suppress the helpless emotion at all costs, or they would arouse people's suspicions. At long last, when it was near sunset, they saw her carry a bucket and head for the stream.

Quickly, they sneaked ahead of her and lay in ambush. Before long, the innocent virgin was caught in a trap of death. The poor woman was abducted and sneaked into the thick bush the instant she got to the hiding place. Before she could make an attempt to sound the alarm, her mouth was tied with Sellotape. Then, as if that was not bad enough, they blindfolded her and afterwards tied her legs and hands with pieces of rope. She was virtually unconscious when they got to the chosen spot.

Coincidentally, Dabi-Dabi had gone hunting for birds and was setting traps in the thick bush to catch wood pigeons. Quite close to the scene of the crime, it suddenly attracted his attention. But he got so scared to death that he decided to sneak away to save his life. Then suddenly, he remembered something that really inspired bravery in him. It was something that Shakespeare had once said: "Cowards die many times before their deaths; the valiant never taste of death but once."

At once, he mustered courage and witnessed the hideous crime in full. In spite of his apparent courage, however, he took fright and shuddered badly as he watched the wolves in sheep's clothing behead the innocent woman in cold blood. Then, as if that was not bad enough, they went ahead and removed her heart pitilessly. Afterwards, they discussed in whispers how best they could guard against suspicion.

Panin: "I suggest we run away and return a few days later."

Nyank: "No, that'd rather arouse people's suspicions. I think we should stay and even join in the search for her when she's finally reported missing."

Kakra: "Good suggestion. But what about the parts?"

Tawia: "We'll take them home and hide them in the freezer until the storm is over."

Panin: "All right, bros, let's get out of here at once."

The criminals left the body at the spot and vanished. But they did not go home straightaway. They suddenly felt it was safer to wait for the gathering darkness to grow fully. So they went deep into the bush and hid there for the time being.

Blissfully unaware, the witness who was still running at speed was now getting close to the palace. The young hunter felt the Chief was the right person to hear about the horrible crime first.

When the Chief whose doors were always open saw the young man materialise from the entrance he got alarmed. "Who's pursuing you, young man?" he asked in puzzlement. But the young man who was now standing before him could not utter a word. He only groaned and panted heavily, shaking his head many times to signal that he was not being pursued.

"Then calm down - calm down and take a seat," the Chief said in a fairly relieved tone. "Just make yourself comfortable and try to recover your composure. Then you can talk to me."

The poor hunter, after groaning and panting for hours, managed to compose himself somewhat. Then he went ahead and recounted everything he had witnessed down to the last detail. Afterwards, he was fed and then asked to stay at the palace pending an immediate action by the Council.

Nana Nifa Dufa, astounded at the vivid eyewitness account, summoned an emergency meeting of the Council in a twinkling. While the brief meeting was underway, the leaders of the two vigilante groups were invited. Of course, they all arrived immediately. And after the news had been broken to them, they were tasked to organise their men for the arrest of the alleged murderers overnight. Meanwhile, they were implored to be vigilant.

Around midnight while the snakes under grass must be fast asleep, the men laid siege to their house in their numbers. They knocked several times on the main door and waited for it to be opened. Strangely, no one did. They knocked harder for a while, ordering the door to be opened at the top of their voices simultaneously. But, still, no one gave any response and no one opened the door either.

Now, the indications were that they had deliberately refused to open the door. Eventually, the men broke in and got the murderers arrested and held to ransom. But as though they were hardened criminals, they flatly refused to get them the hidden treasure despite the prolonged molestation. As a matter of fact, they did not even admit to committing the crime. But after combing and ransacking the whole house for a while, it was finally discovered in the freezer. Of course, they received the beating of their lives after the discovery of the hard evidence. Before they were finally dragged to the palace in chains, their faces were virtually disfigured. In fact, they could hardly be recognised.

The ageing Chief was stupefied, to say the least, when the human parts were shown to him. Although the heinous crime was not something that had never happened before, it was the very first throughout his long years on the Stool. "Lock them in the abandoned guardroom!" he ordered with fury. "They'll be handed over to the police tomorrow morning for the law to take its full course."

"But why did you take the law into your own hands?" he questioned the leaders. "Why did you touch them? Well, be prepared to be answerable to the police."

It took a great while for a verdict to be delivered and everyone felt justice had been delayed. Meanwhile, the mutilated body was still in the mortuary. But no sooner had the agitation intensified than a verdict was eventually returned. Not surprisingly, each of the accused was found guilty of murder and sentenced to life imprisonment in hard labour. Neene, the priest who abetted the crime, was also sent to jail.

Shortly after the sentence had been passed, the awful remains of Abanaba were laid to rest. But prior to that, a series of purification rites were performed by the chief priest. Those customary rites were supposedly meant to placate the earth goddess, the gods and the ancestors for the defilement of their land. Now, the community was rest assured that there would be no resultant calamity.

The gruesome murder of the young virgin, like any other form of murder, was a taboo of the highest order according to tradition. Accordingly, she was not supposed to be mourned at all. So although she was of age and thus deserved normal burial and funeral at least, nothing of the sort happened. The body was just put in the ground. Simply put, she was buried without ceremony.

The sad banishment of the murderers' mother followed hard on the heels of the poor house help's burial. Unknown to her, the decision was taken as soon as the link between the murder and the curse on the family was established. All things considered, the Council of Elders that was chaired by the Chief felt that the woman was a potential threat to the village. They strongly believed that her bad luck as well as her evil machinations could spell doom for the community one day. So they unanimously took the decision that was being put into action today.

The woman was escorted to the Ananse Dokono stream, the southern boundary of the village, and declared persona non grata by the chief priest. Subsequently, the escort returned to the village and left her to fate. Sadly, luck was not on her side. She was shortly murdered in cold blood by an unknown gang. But it could be members of the bereaved family who decided to have their revenge. It could also be people who had taken blood money from the family.

The body of the poor woman, which was virtually decomposed, was later discovered by a group of hunters who were on an expedition. Unfortunately, tradition was not tempered with sentiment and thus the whole village refused to have anything to do with it. So it was probably left at the mercy of scavengers.

Shortly after the sad incident, Yaa-Yaa paid her old friend a visit. It had been ages since they last saw each other. So when she heard the piece of distressing news, she decided to pay her the surprise visit and offer her condolences. But it all turned out to be a mystery piece of news to the bereaved. Auntie Serwaa was stupefied when her friend suddenly broke the news while she was telling her the purpose of the visit. She was totally unaware of the miserable loss as well as her brothers' life imprisonment. As a matter of fact, all the strange happenings in the family were unknown to her.

But something really mysterious, even miraculous, followed the discovery in a twinkling. Strangely enough, Auntie Serwaa suddenly regained her sanity. The woman came to her senses the instant she heard the sad news of her mother's death. Suddenly, she began to wonder why she had all the while abandoned the family that had always loved and supported her. Helpless tears of spontaneous emotion kept running down her remorseful face as she remained inconsolable for a while.

The brief moment was simply eventful. Unbelievably, another miracle had occurred when the woman regained her composure. She realised to her utter surprise that Yaro Baba had disappeared bag and baggage. Every single happening within the short span of the friend's visit was such a drama to behold.

Shortly, Auntie Serwaa went back to the village and reconciled with her father. No doubt the thoughtful move was the surprise of the man's life. He was instantly turned into smiles, and he was likely to remain so forever. Papa Gyabaa was so delighted with the reunion that he never ceased saying thankyou to God, the gods and his ancestors.

Suddenly, the thought struck him to tell the woman about everything that had happened in the family. First and foremost, he explained the aura of mystery that had all the while surrounded her ordeal. He further explained why he could not have the boldness to tell her about it. Then he went ahead and told her about the expedition to the north and everything that happened there. Finally, he told her about the crime and everything else down to the miserable death of her mother.

The glaring omission, however, was the story about the divorce. The man did not even mention it in passing. And although Auntie Serwaa had already heard about it from her friend, she remained incurious. After all, she was there for reconciliation but not to probe. But she could hardly believe the story behind her ordeal which was virtually the only omission in her friend's account. For a moment, she was dumbfounded. Innocent of everything about the deal that led to the curse, she felt that she did not deserve to be going through such a terrible ordeal. But she did not lay the blame on her late mother. Instead, she felt very disappointed in her late grandparents, her late grandmother especially.

Auntie Serwaa was equally displeased with Mother Nature. She felt that suffering the lion's share of the consequences of those late relatives' mistakes was grossly unfair. "I think the immortal goddess shouldn't have remained unconcerned," she said to herself.

In the course of time, the woman and the general manager of her bars who had long been a widower got attracted to each other. Sadly, each of them had personal issues that inhibited the expression of their feelings somehow. The manager, first and foremost, felt he could not risk losing his job. The man felt that the woman may mistake his expressions for disrespect and fire him. His widowhood status too made him feel less confident. But the woman was mainly put off by the strange, recurrent sexual experience with real men.

One moment, the man plucked up courage and asked the woman out, and that was how their enviable relationship began.

Gradually, they found each other compatible and were ready to commit.

Although they were now in a close relationship, no sex had occurred yet. Thus, the woman knew there was still a hurdle to cross. But she crossed her fingers for good luck and before long the obstacle was surmounted. One Friday, the man asked her to sleep over for the very first time and, strangely enough, he could make love to her. And from that moment forward, they were inseparable.

The new lovers did not cohabit. They made timely arrangements and got married. Afterwards, and not surprisingly, the man and his two children, a boy and a girl, moved into the woman's house.

Although the union did not produce any children, the couple still lived happily forever. The woman who was now in her menopause took consolation in her two stepchildren and enjoyed her married life to the full. She proudly regarded them as her own blood and did everything to maintain a tight bond with them. In return for her motherly love and warmth, the children too held her in high esteem. They replaced their late mother with her and loved and cherished her. They treated her like royalty and never did anything to hurt her or betray her trust.

CHAPTER 23

The Escape of the Quadruplets from Prison

The quadruplets went over the top again. They actually proved to be smarter than the security force at the central prison. The place was supposed to be their home forever and ever. But the young men felt they could not live the rest of their lives under restraint. Having been in jail for nearly three years, they had acquainted themselves with the conditions of the place, especially the security measures and their weaknesses. They had learnt that a few teams of warders were rather weak and could be overcome with a determined effort. Quite confident of success, they decided to capitalise on the situation to free themselves. They actually planned their escape and waited patiently for the opportune moment.

The sentence they were serving involved a great deal of hard labour. They were frequently sent out under escort to do one daunting work or another. One morning, they, together with many other convicts, were assigned to a construction company. The company had been contracted by the Prisons Service to build new quarters for the senior staff of the central branch. It had requested the assistance of the prisoners to enable it complete the project on, or ahead of, schedule.

Presently, the structure they occupied was a death trap. The authorities were therefore in a great hurry to relocate them to forestall disaster. So the contractor was under intense pressure to fast-track the completion of the project.

Unfortunately, it all turned out to be a journey of no return for both the workhorses and the escort. While they were returning in the evening, the thought struck the brothers to seize the opportunity to carry out their agenda. It was getting dusky and the place was somewhat lonely. Again, the road was least busy. Convinced that the escort was quite weak and could be overcome, they decided to mount an attack to facilitate their escape. They quickly reasoned non-verbally with the others and had their instant support. Then suddenly, they pounced on the escort, seized control and succeeded in killing all of them. They were six in number, including three females and three males. Even the unarmed driver's life was not spared in the desperate attack that was masterminded by the quadruplet brothers.

Now, it was time to run for their lives and, as if by magic, they all vanished in the twinkling of an eye. They fled in groups and individually in every direction without any specific destinations.

Shortly, the barbaric attack made the headlines and remained so for days. But all the overwhelming publicity as well as the frantic search by the police proved futile. None of the escapees was rearrested. The Police Service in collaboration with the Prisons Service even went as far as to promise any informants a fortune. But everything was just a vain effort. The criminals had actually vanished from the face of the earth.

"They've probably crossed the borders to any of the neighbouring countries," one serial caller said during a radio phone-in. "Otherwise, the king's ransom alone would have produced many informants." But the majority felt they were still hiding in the country.

After almost a year of fruitless efforts to apprehend the fugitives, the police virtually gave up the ghost. Every-thing was seemingly abandoned.

Having gone into hiding all the while, the quadruplets had finally settled in Kwasaasa. The hiding place, a very remote and deprived village, was somewhere in the west. They had now turned over a new leaf and decided to pick up the pieces. Each of them actually appeared changed, both in appearance and behaviour.

The 'innocent' quadruplets appeared in the peaceful village one evening. The generous Chief gladly accepted them into the community on behalf of the hospitable people. He even lived with them in his cottage until their permanent accommodation was ready. With the wholehearted support of the entire village, their sizeable mud hut was built within a fortnight.

Although they were new settlers, they did not fold their arms. They did their utmost to make a living without burdening the hospitable people so much. They worked hard on people's farms and plantations and got paid. They also did many other menial jobs to earn some money. So they were able to maintain themselves without much difficulty. But they lived principally on charity.

Gradually, the new crop season finally began, and not a moment too soon. It really promised to be good, judging by the frequency of rain as well as the high intensity of the sun. Everyone was poised to take full advantage of it and the quadruplet brothers were without exception. In actual fact, they resolved to capitalise on the vast expanse of farmland at their disposal to become independent after the season.

The men made a very big farm and cultivated a great variety of crops. Luckily for them and the entire village for that matter, what they anticipated became a reality. The season was truly wonderful. The rain was reliable and temperatures were conducive too. Soon, the farms were all beautiful and a marvel to behold. The whole village was counting the days to a good harvest. The quadruplets especially remained expectant.

Panin: "So how are we going to manage the produce after harvest, bros?"

Tawia: "Oh no! First things first, Panin. I think it's too early to think about that. We'd better concern ourselves with how the big dream could be realised."

Kakra: "But the signs are as clear as day, Tawia! The frequent rain, the high temperatures, the state of the farm now, you name it. There's surely a good harvest ahead!"

Panin: "Well, bros, we simply can't afford to have a bad harvest. We'd better be positive, every last of us."

Nyank: "Sure, optimism is our watchword henceforth. We're definitely going to have nothing but a good harvest. But we can't reckon without low prices for farm produce."

Kakra: "That's a point. Since there's going to be a bumper harvest, produce will have to be sold off, or they'll just rot. And that means income will be marginal."

Nyank: "So what should our prayer be?"

Panin: "Very simple! A good harvest for us and a bad one for our neighbours!"

Tawia: "But that won't be fair, Panin. We just can't wish our neighbours ill. They've been very welcoming and helpful."

Panin: "So what do you suggest, Good Samaritan?"

Tawia: "The answer is preservation, bros. We must find means for preserving our produce for good prices - that's all."
Nyank: "You've really got a point, Tawia. Preservation seems a better suggestion."
The others: "Hear! Hear!"
Panin: "Unique Brothers!"
The others: "Together we act, divided we don't!"

The quadruplets remained anxious for a good harvest, only to see the mystery of their lives in the end. Unbelievably, no single crop on the big farm even flowered, let alone yielded anything. None of the maize produced grains, and none of the cassava or yam produced tubers either. Again, none of the vegetable plants and the other crops produced anything.

The outlandish experience, obviously without precedent in the annals of farming in the village and beyond, fuelled a lot of speculation. The popular one was the belief that the gods of the land probably disapproved of the men's acceptance into the community. What even added to the perplexity of the incident was the general bumper harvest in the village. Every single farm had a record harvest. So it was a truly baffling situation and perhaps the popular speculation was not untenable.

The men remained perplexed for a while. They could not even find a probable cause for the weird experience. They eventually attributed it to misfortune and hoped for good luck in the ensuing season. But they kept wondering about how the people genuinely felt about it and how they would behave towards them as a result. They were also worried about living off them until the next crop season. No one had yet behaved strangely towards them, though.

One moment while they talked worriedly about the eerie incident, something crossed Tawia's mind. But the third of the quadruplets refused to share it immediately. Instead, he decided to keep it to himself for the meantime. Perhaps he did not want to rub salt in a wound.

Months passed by and a few incidents took place. But what happened to the quadruplets still remained the talk of the village. The men themselves couldn't get over the mystery. They remained eaten up by it for long. Quite apart from the fact that they found it fathomless, they did not know how to check its recurrence. Of course, they could ill afford to see it happen again. In the midst of the desperation, Tawia decided to share the thought he had harboured all the while.

Tawia: "I've been contemplating why the eerie experience came about for some time. Don't you think it's got something to do with the curse?"
Nyank: "Wait a minute! That's a point! I think the facts speak for themselves."
Panin: "You never said a truer word, Tawia. That curse is nothing short of bad luck."

Kakra: "So what do we do?"
Tawia: "Why don't we sleep on it and take the best decision tomorrow or some other time, bros?"
Panin: "I think you've got a point. What do you think, bros?"
The others: "Hear! Hear!"

Shortly, the men visited Kankra Kaden, the great fetish in Pomposo. It was about an eighteen-kilometre journey on foot from the hideout. A Samaritan, a hunter they met by chance who had apparently been there before, recommended the place to them. The veteran priest called them to 'the consulting room' and attended to them promptly.

Priest: "The linkage you made between the strange incident and the curse on your family was wrong, young men. You can no longer ascribe your misfortunes to it, for it has been reversed without trace. I do not intend to reopen old wounds, but your late mother did what was expected of her in the land of the dead. Her ghost and that of the herbalist to whom she was betrothed after birth got married and afterwards the curse was reversed. So the family, I mean you and your only sister, has since had its freedom."
Panin: "So if I may ask, Nana, who or what was responsible for the strange experience?"

Priest: "The crimes you have committed have caught up with you spiritually, young men. You must confess them to Nana Kankra Kaden now. Then he can intercede with the spirits behind the strange incident on your behalf."
Panin: "With all due respect, Nana, what crimes are you talking about? I cannot remember anything of that sort. Or can any of you, Unique Brothers?"
The others: "Emm, emm…… No, Panin."
Panin: "There is nothing to confess, Nana. We have not committed any crime against anyone."

The priest, surprised at the blatant lie, gave them the evil eye and then said: "Well, young men, Great Kaden cannot offer any form of help to shameless liars like you. So you may leave and come back whenever you are ready to confess to him. But you must prepare for more of the misfortunes henceforth. Your stubborn streak has enraged the great spirit."

Suddenly, their faces clouded over in awe and confusion, betraying a hidden secret somehow. But it seemed that the confession they were expected to make was undecided. So they asked permission and left, their senses of unease boldly written on their faces.

CHAPTER 24

Struggling for Survival

On their way back, the criminals who were at large talked at length about the lie Panin told the priest on their behalf. They spoke in an undertone as much as possible.

Kakra: "But why did you unilaterally decide to tell a lie on our behalf, Panin?"

The others: "We just wonder why he did that."

Panin: "It was for our own safety, bros. Or you expected me to tell the truth and cause our exposure?"

Tawia: "But I don't think telling that man the truth would have meant running the risk of arrest, Panin. I'm told that the position of such people compels them to be secretive."

Nyank: "That's quite right, bros. I'm told that every traditional priest is made to take an oath of secrecy as part of their ordination."

Panin: "Well, better safe than sorry, bros. I don't think it'll be advisable to take a gamble on confiding in that man. I still insist we let sleeping dogs lie."
Tawia: "But sleeping dogs can't lie still when they're endangered, Panin. As per what the man said, our lives are still in danger despite the refusal to confess. So we'd better take the risk of confessing everything to him."
Nyank: "I think he's got a point, bros. Confession seems inevitable."
Kakra: "But it isn't too late yet, bros. We can still go back and do what we're supposed to do."
Panin: "Ei, bros! There's no such thing as trust in situations such as this-oo! We'd better think twice-oo! Mmm!"
Tawia: "There's no cause for alarm, big bro."
Panin: "Unique Brothers!"
The others: "Together we act, divided we don't!"
Panin: "Well, it's obvious we're divided over this issue and thus there'll be no confession, at least not now."
The others: "Hear! Hear!"

Panin continued to take issues with his brothers about the confession for quite a while. But he eventually succeeded in convincing them to have a change of mind. Then they finalised that confession was completely out of the possibilities.

Having ruled out confession, the men seemed prepared for any eventuality now. But the experiences that ensued the bold decision were terrifying. They only prompted a lot more speculation about what they must really be. The popular opinion was that the brothers were either evil or cursed with misfortunes. Consequently, they were treated with contempt and made to suffer all forms of abuse and humiliation. Virtually all the people shunned them. And as if that was not bad enough, they were either mocked or sneered at by whoever they met or passed by.

Only a handful of the people still hired them to work on their farms. And only a few Samaritans were willing to lend them their farm implements and other things. The unlucky men were practically ostracised. But they managed to endure the rejection and remained adamant about the confession. But for how long could they hold to their decision in the midst of the nightmarish experiences? Well, anyway, the drama continued to unfold.

One afternoon, they went hunting in the nearby forest as usual. Game had always been their chief source of meat and perhaps the whole village's. All of a sudden, Panin spotted a big antelope at close quarters. Quickly, he held on to the double-barrelled gun and took aim almost simultaneously. "Powaa! Powaa!" he fired two shots and killed it instantly. "Come with me, bros!" he called out delightedly. "We shall have a feast this evening!"

They all hurried there in great delight and surrounded the game as usual. Then they felt it in turn.

"We shall cook 'fufu' and 'kontomire' soup for supper, bros," Kakra said. "The game will best go with that."

"You have a strong sense of taste, bro," Nyank gave a compliment.

"Thanks," he replied. "But don't forget I'm the chief cook."

"But what're we still waiting for, bros?" Tawia said. "We'd better carry it home now."

Indeed, wonders will never cease. The instant two of the men made an attempt to lift the dead animal by the feet, something shocking as well as mystifying happened. It suddenly turned into the mutilated corpse of the poor virgin they murdered. "Christ!" they exclaimed in chorus and bolted in all directions. But they eventually found themselves running along the footpath that led to the village, each of them trying very hard to run past the other. It was such a funny running contest.

No doubt about it, the escapees who had disguised themselves as people seeking their fortune were doomed to misery. Otherwise, they would not be plagued by misfortunes. But why did terrible misfortunes never cease to befall them? There was another mystery when they got home. Although there had not been any storm, the thatched roof of their hut had ripped off completely. Oh what another bizarre incident!

The entire village raised their eyebrows in disbelief, and their suspicions were quickly aroused. Suddenly, everyone began to call them names. Whereas the majority branded them evil, the rest felt they were just hoodoo. But whichever name or description they deemed fit, that only added to the insinuation and rejection.

Presently, none of the people wanted to have anything to do with them again. Most people even wished they could avoid talking to them, greeting them, even. The women especially loathed seeing them around. They felt that they were a real threat to their peace and security as well as their children's. No doubt they would have chased them out of the village if they had their way.

The whole village felt insecure living with the mysterious men. They felt that their presence could spell doom for them one day. After all, what they had witnessed so far was more than enough evidence. Apparently, the 'evil' men were still being tolerated somewhat on humanitarian grounds. The people probably didn't go to extremes because of their hallmark of hospitality. But even so, the men were made to feel more unwelcome.

The rejection the quadruplets suffered did not only tell on their emotions but also on their feeding. Had it not been for the little food they obtained from people's old farms, they would have gone hungry. But they regularly searched those abandoned farms and got some little foodstuffs and mushrooms and suchlike food with which they maintained themselves. And although the people were well aware they fed from that source, they never forbade them from doing so. Obviously, the grounds were humanitarian again.

Hunting had always been their main source of meat. But the last experience had virtually brought the everyday activity to a halt. It had actually put each of them off handling the gun again. They now saw the tool as the scariest object in the whole wide world. Thus, they had opted for trap setting, but even so they were very cautious about trapping dangerous game.

Unluckily, the new means for hunting failed to be a better alternative. The traps mostly caught inedible game, most of which were really dangerous. They frequently caught cobras and pythons and suchlike wild animals. Even some of them would still be alive whenever they went to check on the traps. But such animals, apart from being dangerous, were either unwholesome or inedible at all as per their cultural norms and values. Eventually, the poor quadruplets felt they could not dice with death and thus abandoned the method altogether. Thenceforth, snails and mushrooms became substitutes for meat.

One afternoon, the men went hunting for snails and mushrooms to prepare supper with. Luckily for them, Panin soon came across a cluster of the former that were circling slowly around a pawpaw tree. They were seven in number, quite big in size and appealing. At once, he called out to his brothers to come along. They were all there in seconds to have a glimpse of what their elder brother had seen. Standing close to the tree and watching the wonderful scene in awe, each of them made interesting comments to express how fascinated they were. Then suddenly, the excitement was replaced by shock.

"Christ!" they yelled in chorus at the top of their voices, fleeing in different directions simultaneously. The main necessaries for the evening meal had turned into something else. They had changed into the bodies of the six warders and the driver whom they brutally murdered one fateful evening.

The latest incident too was nothing less than another wake-up call to them to do the right thing. At least they had been frightened enough and given a reason to bite the bullet. But did they yield? Certainly not! They remained as adamant as ever. They did not even consider the option. The decision on the confession seemed very tenacious indeed.

Rather certainly, the picture would have been different if they had the freedom to decide individually. Strongly conditioned by solidarity since childhood, they may have felt compelled to remain united at all costs. Even their slogan said it all. In fact, departing from precedent seemed unlikely, if not impossible.

The fear of being turned against, harmed or eliminated could also explain their unshakable unity. Any disloyal brother, any of them with opposing views for that matter, was likely to be considered an enemy and dealt with. Although they loved each other and were inseparable, the tendency for hostility towards any such brother could not be ruled out. The secrecy of the hideous crimes they had committed and their safety for that matter could be of paramount importance.

Unknown to them, of course, their father had been sick and bedridden for quite a long time. Now, he had finally died a few weeks ago and had even been buried. Their rich sister had single-handedly sponsored a grand funeral to mourn him. Having missed the opportunity to bury her late mother, she probably felt compelled to make her father's a memorable ceremony.

Auntie Serwaa, ostensibly honouring her late father by the grand funeral, was actually showing off her riches. No wonder there were raised eyebrows at the extent of the ostentation. Some people, the poor especially, even felt that it was sheer waste of the scarce paper. But the majority, including most of the bereaved family, felt it was reasonable extravagance and were full of praise for the woman. The whole of Kunso had enough to eat and drink. In fact, the funeral was more of feasting than mourning. But behind the praise and admiration were concerns about the dying out of the family. Now her parents were dead and the quadruplets were not likely to return, everyone felt it was near dissolution.

CHAPTER 25

The Eventual Confession

B ack in Kwasaasa, the misfortunes had not ceased befalling the mysterious quadruplets yet. All the people were now bored with the strange happenings. They felt that the safety of the village could no longer be compromised in the name of hospitality. There was thus a massive outcry against the Chief and the Elders for their seeming unconcern and inaction.

The ensuing eerie occurrences were real Doomsday scenarios and the straw that broke the camel's back. Some young women went to fetch water from Ahinam, the most preferred source of drinking water, one evening. They happened to meet the quadruplet brothers there. They were busily scooping some of the water into their pots with their calabashes. The women sat on the bench of rock at the bank and waited their turn. Then, as if by magic, the quadruplets' hands got stuck in the stream simultaneously.

"Help! Help! Help!" they shouted in chorus. Alarmed though, the women gathered some courage, drew closer and stretched their necks like giraffes to satisfy their curiosity. To their amazement, the water in the stream had turned into blood and that in the pots likewise. At once, they all left their pots behind and ran back to the village to sound the alarm.

All the men in the village ran there at speed to see everything for themselves. Lo and behold, the men were screaming for help at the top of their voices when they got there. And just as it had been reported, the stream had truly turned blood.

Shocked and petrified at the same time, everyone stood at a distance and observed the mystery with an apparent sense of detachment. Then after some time, everything suddenly returned to normality. The bloody stream turned pure again and before long the men were freed.

But the people remained unconvinced about the purity of the water in the stream. They felt that it was no longer safe for drinking and other domestic use. Having interpreted the mystery superstitiously, no one ever fetched water from that source again.

The following day was a Wednesday. While all the youth had gathered in the morning for communal labour as usual, they suddenly saw a cloud of smoke in the sky. It was huge and clearly suggestive of an outbreak of fire. Quickly, they traced it to the source and, not surprisingly, it had to do with the 'evil' men again. Their new farm had caught fire and was burning violently. Strangely enough, the fire did not spread beyond the boundaries of the farm. Although everything in it got burnt into ashes, none of the farms that shared boundaries with it got affected. That was actually the air of mystery about the occurrence. No one seemed too confounded by it, though. After all, the quadruplets were now synonymous with strange happenings in the village.

However, everyone became increasingly agitated. All things considered, they felt that the time to chase the mysterious men out of the place was long overdue. "Enough is enough," they said to each other. The women in particular were more impatient. Vulnerable and their children likewise, they knew they were the ones who would suffer most should any calamity occur. Thus, they felt obliged to do all they could to forestall any such situation.

All of them, single or married, gathered in the evening for a peaceful demonstration. The bold move was intended for the Chief and the Elders of the village especially. It was meant to press them into driving 'the evil men', as they put it, out of the peaceful village at once. Starting from the market where they met, the bevy of concerned women paraded peacefully through the whole village. As they walked on, they chanted: "They must leave or we shall leave! They are hoodoo! They are evil! They must go! They must leave now!"

The women ended everything in front of the Chief's cottage. While they kept chanting the threat louder now, a group of Elders came out to calm them down. But it took a great while for them to become fairly composed. Then, painstakingly and rather eloquently, their spokesperson presented their verbal petition to the Chief through the men. The voice of the women was primarily a plea. It pleaded with the Chief to ask 'the evil men' to leave the village for it to regain its tranquil setting.

The following morning, as early as possible, the Chief and all the Elders trooped to the quadruplets' house. "You must leave this place immediately," the Chief ordered. "We can no longer tolerate your misfortunes. The whole village - the young, the old and us - are sick with fear because of your calamitous fate. You must leave now, or else you'll be chased away."

"Please, take pity on us, Nana and Elders of Kwasaasa," Panin pleaded. "No doubt your actions are justifiable. But we still plead with you to be merciful. We have nowhere to go if you drive us out."

"You deserve no mercy!" the Chief said quite severely. "Enough is enough!"

No amount of impassioned plea could make the Chief who had the full support of his people have a change of mind. So the men had no alternative but to leave the place for good. They hesitantly packed up and soon left the village. But before they finally did, they were sternly warned against setting foot there again.

Stranded and racked by indecision and despair, they slowly stalked away from the forbidden land. Sadly, they had no particular destination. They just walked on and on and eventually found themselves in a thick forest. In the obviously dangerous forest where they were wandering, the men felt tired, thirsty and hungry. They were virtually exhausted. At the same time they felt their lives were particularly endangered.

Tawia: "We'd better be more reasonable now, bros, or we'll be dead and gone shortly. And, clearly, we'll have no good story to tell."

Nyank: "My sentiments exactly, Tawia. Something really needs to be done urgently."

Kakra: "So what're you two driving at?"

Tawia: "I think we've got no other option but to go back to Pomposo and confess to the priest."

Nyank: "Sure! Obviously, there can't be any better alternative now."

Kakra: "You never said a truer word, bros. What do you think, Panin?"

Panin: "I beg your pardon, bros! We can't take any regrettable decision just because we're desperate! We'd best be wise and let things lie."

Tawia: "I think it's high time you changed your entrenched feelings about the confession, the obvious panacea to our sufferings, Panin. We can't continue to deceive ourselves, for goodness' sake. You'd best back the right horse, big bro."

Kakra: "Well, Panin, as you can see, the three of us make up the majority. And the majority, as they say, carries the day. So it's a win for us but a loss for you on this occasion. We're confessing at once."

Panin: "Fair enough! But how do we get there?"

Tawia: "Now you've come to your senses, big bro! Oh well, anyhow, back to the question, I think the answer is quite obvious. We'll sneak to the village in the dead of the night and take the path we know."

Panin: "And how do we survive between now and then? I mean, what do we live on?"

Kakra: "Oh drop the bombardment, big bro! We'll have to survive the same way we would if there hasn't been a change of mind about the confession."

Nyank: "That's quite enough, bros. We'd better start searching for wild fruits and nuts and possibly a source of water."

The others: Hear! Hear!"

The inseparable quadruplets were at the place the following morning ready to confess the atrocious crimes they had committed. They were quite apprehensive, having thought that the seasoned priest would be very angry with them. But their thoughts turned out to be mere imaginings. The man was even more friendly and welcoming now. After listening to their incredible story, however, there was a mood swing. Speechless, no doubt, he remained dumb for a while before he finally decided to offer help.

Priest: "Well, you will stay here for the meantime, young men. You will be fed and sheltered free of charge while you undergo thorough purification and then fortification. Afterwards, you can go back to Kwasaasa. The people will surely welcome you back and show you the hospitality you deserve."
Panin: "Thank you very much, Nana. But, please, how do we pay for your services?"
Priest: "You will pay the humble servant of the great fetish in cash. But you can defer payment until you are ready. After all, your well-being is the priority of Kankra Kaden the Great and his loyal servant. I really sympathise with you in your present circumstance."
The brothers: "Thank you very much, Nana. We shall forever remain indebted to you."
Priest: "That's all right."

One good turn, as they say, deserves another. On the third day, after they had gone through the ritual of purification in the morning, the men offered to go to farm with the generous priest. They strongly felt the need to do any work that needed to be done there.

The quadruplet brothers really worked their fingers to the bone in return for the man and his household's hospitality. They virtually finished every work on the sizeable crop farm before they returned home in the evening.

A very fat goat was slaughtered and used to cook supper for the family. The palatable meal, 'fufu' and groundnut soup, was very probably a special treat for the quadruplets. In any case, it was incidentally their favourite. The aroma alone was irresistible, not to talk of the taste and the garnishing. The men who were sincerely appreciative of the generous gesture really did justice to the food. They ate all the five balls that were served them and even asked for more. As a matter of fact, they ate the family out of house and home.

About a week later, when the supposed purification and fortification rites were almost done with, there occurred a startling twist of fortune. At the crack of dawn while the men were still fast asleep, they heard a gentle knock on the door. Although each of them heard the unusual knock, everyone felt too lazy to respond and open the door. They all pretended as though they did not hear anything. But the person kept knocking mildly harder until Nyank hesitantly got out of bed and opened the door.

"Christ!" he exclaimed in utter disbelief. "We're dead, bros!"

"What's it?" the others asked in chorus, rushing to the door as one to satisfy their curiosity.

"We're finished!" they said together.

Blissfully unaware, the smart priest had sneaked to the district police station and reported them. So while they had the wishful thinking that they were now secure and had gone unpunished for that matter, they were gradually being put in the grip of the law.

"You have every right to remain silent," one policeman said, "for whatever you say here may be used as evidence against you in the court of law."

"Handcuff every one of them and follow them into the car," another policeman, probably the highest in command, ordered.

As the Police Service had promised, the patriotic priest was handsomely rewarded for the wonderfully orchestrated arrest. Again, he suddenly rose to prominence.

The quadruplets were re-arraigned on two charges of multiple murder and unlawful escape from the grip of the law. They were accordingly sentenced to death by hanging. The capital punishment was scheduled to take place on the fourteenth day from the day of the verdict.

Having received nationwide publicity, Auntie Serwaa was acutely aware of both the re-arrest of her brothers and the death penalty. The same held true for the extended family and the townspeople at large. The woman was sick at heart about the horrible death that awaited her brothers. She could neither eat nor drink anything, and she could not think straight either. In fact, she was terribly hurt.

"Misfortunes and the pain and trauma that come with them have been the story of my life," she said tearfully one moment. "Why me, Mother Nature? Why me, for goodness' sake?"

Her loving husband and stepchildren were grief-stricken too, especially about her distraught state. They couldn't stand to see her moan and sigh pathetically in grief.

The heartbreaking commentary on the death sentence was what even compounded her depression. Most of it was clearly unsupported and simply derogatory in the opinion of the heartbroken sister. Most of the arguments wrongly implicated innocent people in the crimes. Every member of the family was unfairly connected to them and even abused verbally. That popular attitude, in her opin-ion, was uninformed and uncalled for and thus sickening.

But such condemnatory comments about crimes, murder especially, were not unusual. The Ama Ghana society frowned upon crimes and all forms of illegality for that matter. But murder was detested. Murderers were treated beneath contempt and their families were without exception. So it was clearly wrong but commonplace for people to react to the issue the way they did.

All too soon, today, a Friday, was the last day on earth for the condemned prisoners. No doubt they were despairingly counting down the minutes. Perhaps no one pitied them apart from their sister, their only true family now. The popular feeling was that they had been too cruel to others and thus deserved even the worst punishment. Some people even believed the criminals themselves must have felt at some point or another that they truly deserved to die. But their downhearted sister thought otherwise. She felt that they still deserved to live and that the death penalty was inhuman.

But was there any objectivity in Auntie Serwaa's argument? Well, in any case, the die was cast and neither the sentiment nor the fuss could make any difference.

A sense of pending doom engulfed the woman throughout the day. She refused to eat or drink anything and only remained restless. Her husband and stepchildren who genuinely or otherwise shared her sentiment kept her company all day and tried to console her. But she remained inconsolable.

At last, the execution was broadcast on the national television channel on the evening news. Auntie Serwaa, on seeing the disturbing or rather the horrendous sketches of the execution of her brothers, passed out at once. She was rushed to the nearest hospital but was instantly referred to the Kofi Annan Military Hospital where she was admitted. Poor Auntie Serwaa remained in intensive care for weeks. Sadly, she could not make it. She was eventually pronounced dead in coma.

The woman's death was a real blow to her husband who was rendered a widower again. Her stepchildren too were devastated, having been left motherless again. In fact, the family never stopped grieving over the loss.

Jointly with the extended family, they gave her befitting burial and funeral. Afterwards, they mounted a bust of her in front of her magnificent house to her memorial.

Glossary

Abusuapanin	the head of an extended family
Allah	God
Awo	a response to a greeting
Borgar	someone who lives abroad or has been there before
bragoro	initiation rites for girls at Puberty
bro/bros	brother/brothers
Ei	an exclamation expressing disbelief
fufu	a dish prepared by pounding cassava and plantain into balls
gari	cassava flour roasted into coarse grains
Insha Allah	God willing
kente	a hand-woven local cloth
kontomire	a leafy green vegetable
Maame/Mma	a title for a woman

Nana	a title for a chief, an old man or woman, or a traditional priest or priestess
Nananom	Elders
Okyeame/'Kyeame	Linguist
'Sante	a way of saying 'Asante', an ethnic group in Ghana
Uui	an exclamation that is more or less a cliché in West Gonja